KT-502-980

Descended from the same North-East family as Robert Burns, Jack Webster was born and brought up in Aberdeenshire. He started his newspaper career in Turriff before moving on to the Aberdeen Journals and later the Express empire of Lord Beaverbrook. He then joined the *Sunday Standard*, and is now a columnist on the *Glasgow Herald*.

Jack Webster's books include *The Dons*, a history of Aberdeen Football Club, and *Gordon Strachan*, the biography of the Aberdeen, Manchester United and Scotland football star. His first attempt at writing for television was the 1986 award-winning film which took the title of the first part of his autobiography, *A Grain of Truth*, and told the story of the final day at his father's farm at Maud.

Jack Webster is married and has three sons, all in journalism.

ANOTHER GRAIN
OF TRUTH

Jack Webster

FONTANA/Collins

First published in Great Britain by
William Collins Sons & Co. Ltd 1988
First issued in Fontana Paperbacks in 1989

Copyright © Jack Webster 1988

Printed and bound in Great Britain by
William Collins Sons & Co. Ltd, Glasgow

To the folk of Buchan,
whose life and language, rich and expressive,
have compelled me to write about them
over the years.

ACKNOWLEDGEMENTS

For permission to quote various items, I would like to thank Colin MacLean of Aberdeen University Press and the Charles Murray Trust; Nora Coutts, David Clark and the newspaper empires of Geo. Outram, Thomson and the Express. Thanks also to Messrs Aitken and Stone for the arrangement to reproduce a passage from *The Kingdom by the Sea* by Paul Theroux. Photographic assistance from George Dey, Leslie Yuill, Forshaw Photographics of Peterhead, Ken Melvin of Glasgow, Scotpix of Aberdeen and Mrs Bennett of Strichen Library was also much appreciated.

CONTENTS

CHAPTER ONE

The Way In . . .

On a wild November afternoon of 1981 I drove up from the south and out through Aberdeen towards the Buchan fishing port of Fraserburgh, a town in which I was far from being a stranger.

I had grown up in that North-East corner of Scotland, just fifteen miles inland, but now I was back as an author for my first real encounter with the 'signing session', that precarious adventure in book promotion which can boost your sales and morale at one deft stroke or send you scurrying for a hiding-place with a colourful attack of embarrassment.

Vivid in my mind was the day I accompanied the American best-selling author, Burt Hirschfeld, to a signing session at which not a single soul turned up. The bookshop manager was reduced to dressing up his staff in overcoats so that they could masquerade as customers and avoid the worst rigours of a total fiasco.

Having driven into the hard blast of an early winter's day in Fraserburgh, where the wind has a habit of reaching parts too private for words as well as comfort, I warmed myself with a plate of Willie Bannerman's broth at the Alexandra Hotel and wondered who would be foolhardy enough to venture out on a day like this for the dubious privilege of attaching my undistinguished signature to their copy of a book I had just written.

Still worse in this moment of self-doubt, what right did I have to expect that there was even a market for this particular type of book, which was, after all, no more than the reminiscences of an Aberdeenshire country boy? I had called it *A Grain of Truth* and publisher Paul Harris had travelled north to Fraserburgh (or the Broch, as I had more commonly known it), anxious to gauge the potential of this sort of literature.

When the broth and the brisket had been well and truly digested we ventured cautiously round the corner of Mid Street in the direction of Mrs Maitland's bookshop, there to behold a sight which did our hearts a power of good. For the queue of customers was already out through the shop and into the winter bleakness of the street. Within the next few hours I had signed no fewer than 270 copies of *A Grain of Truth*, drawing to a halt only because there were no more copies there to sell. We fixed a date for a second session at the same shop, convinced at least that our modest little adventure was not without its public demand.

But commercial considerations were furthest from my mind that memorable afternoon as people came by with stories to tell, sometimes of my own childhood and even that of my parents. By the time I had completed the signing circuit, taking in my native village of Maud and the nearby town of Turriff, where I had started my newspaper career in 1948, I had been through an emotional wringer in the most pleasurable of fashions.

Within those columns of familiar Buchan faces there was the lady who remembered my father, the ebullient John Webster, as a schoolboy pursuing his ambition to be an auctioneer, standing on his mother's kitchen table at the farm of Backhill of Allathan, rouping everything within sight – including his own mother!

There was the formidable daughter of Robbie Paterson, owner of the legendary Turra Coo, who stalked in to say that, along with every other person who had written about that notorious creature, I did not get the story quite right. I met former schoolmates, girl-friends and dancing partners as well as elderly ladies who remembered me in my pram. At Fraserburgh there was the lady who thrust into my hand a snapshot from 1927, when she was a nurse at the City Hospital, Aberdeen, and there I beheld a cheery group of her fellow-nurses which included the carefree and unmistakable figure of Meg Barron, my late mother. That choked me up for the moment and, as the lady too bit back a tear, she turned and vanished before I had time to know her name.

Touching incidents had been happening from the day we launched *A Grain of Truth* at the Aberdeen Art Gallery, where the company included Miss Catto, the infant teacher who welcomed me on that very first day at Maud School in April of 1936, and her colleague, Miss Morrison, who took over in my primary years. It was not an occasion for fancy speeches, but on the spur of the moment Miss Morrison, now Mrs Reith from Banchory, rose to say a few words that were simple and sincere, observing that her former pupil 'has inherited his mother's sentiment and romance and his father's determination'. It was a fair assessment.

The author and one-time farm servant, David Toulmin, was among others who helped to launch *A Grain of Truth* on that Guy Fawkes Day of 1981, a date which prompted the wish that the book might rocket to success rather than fizzle out as a damp squib. I need hardly have worried. The second print had to be ordered before publication day was over, and soon there was not an unsold copy to be found.

In time it gave its title to an award-winning television film, produced by the BBC, and that, in turn, set off a demand for another book. In the avalanche of letters which descended on my desk after two showings of the film, there were some which blossomed into verse, like that of Mrs Ruth Gatt from Bagrae of Alvah, Banff, whom I had once known as Ruth Brodie from Balthangie.

Summing up the essence of the mail in general, she wrote: 'We left our television sets in silence, a lump in our throats, yet proud to belong to that part of Aberdeenshire called Buchan.' She closed with these lines:

> As journalist and North-East loon
> Ye're bra well kent for miles aroon
> Ye've interviewed baith great an' sma
> Seen Honeyneuk fit deep in sna
> 'A Grain o' Truth' ye've written tee

> – An' it taks pride o place wi me –
> So creep in tae yer ingle-neuk
> An' write for's a' – anither beuk.

I have laboured into the night at that 'ingle-neuk' (now fired by gas instead of peat); but if the effort can bring some warmth to the caul blast of a winter's evening, I shall not have gone unrewarded.

CHAPTER TWO

The Roup

When the cameras stopped whirring and the last of the folk had drained away from the farm-close of Honeyneuk that calm summer evening, I wandered round the back of the steading for one last look across the valley of the Ugie towards the woods of Brucklay.

At last I was alone on a day of torn emotion, the day I had finally sold off my father's farm in the heart of that Aberdeenshire cattle country known as Buchan and witnessed the dispersal of his livestock and implements to the winks and nods which he himself would have been the first to detect, in his eventful career as one of the best-known auctioneers in Scotland.

The BBC had chosen the occasion to make a television documentary film of the roup (a Scottish term for an auction sale) and the presence of the camera crew was to add an extra dimension of drama to a day in my life when that commodity would not have been in short supply in any case.

Having long since left the rural scene of my childhood, in physical terms at least, I was back this day to conclude an agonizing decision and to be invited in for my tea at a farmhouse table where my mother had long been the welcoming mistress and my father the indisputable master.

As the new owners of Honeyneuk's 200 acres, Jim and Belinda Muir had already moved in, having uprooted themselves from the Orkney island of Shapinsay and boarded a lorry, together with their two children, dog, cats, hens, bees and assorted goods and chattels for the crossing to the Mainland of Orkney and thereafter for the longer voyage to the landfall of Scotland. That family adventure of a lifetime had brought them through Aberdeenshire and finally into the heart of Buchan, to which many an Orcadian farmer and his family had drifted before them, attracted by the proximity to suppliers and markets and the educational opportunities of which their children might wish to avail themselves in years to come.

So the Muirs had ventured through the front door of Honeyneuk, a house left gaunt and empty with my father and mother both dead and gone, but once a bustling hive of activity, well charged with the power of John Webster's personality and the warmth of my mother's welcoming fly-cup, not to mention her music which pervaded every corner and filtered down the half-mile distance to the village of Maud below.

From that same front door, the Muirs would look beyond the rooftops of Maud and absorb their first exhilarating view of that valley of the Ugie which curled its way from the back of Honeyneuk, round by the Buchan railway line and on towards the Garden of Buchan at Old Deer, eventually to the North Sea at Peterhead.

This was their new beginning in an alien part of Scotland which was to me as familiar as the back of my own hand, the shallow valleys where I had grown up all those years ago, without knowing that I was amassing a wealth of experience, physical, emotional and artistic, which would one day leave me the residual inheritance of my best memories.

Such memories were vividly with me now, in the summer of 1985, as I faced the fact that, for the first time in my fifty-four years, I did not have a place to lay my head in the *quoad sacra* parish of Maud, where I was born.

Jim Muir and his family had settled into the farmhouse of Honeyneuk, just as my parents had done in 1952, and Willie Paul had done before them and the Raes before that, stretching back to the Galls, who had lived in the old farmhouse (later a henhouse) before they built the present one in 1910. Old Sandy Horne from the village would wander past and tell us of how he had been a mason at the building of our substantial dwelling in those early years of the century. Snapshots at the time of building show a bare landscape, as yet without the benefit of nature's artistry which would in time paint in the trees and hedges and terraced garden to make it an enclosure for rhubarb and rhododendrons, kail, cabbage and croquet – and the little summer-house where my mother could toss back her hair, turn her face to the sunshine she adored and dream the dreams which spilled from her romantic nature.

As my former schoolteacher, Miss Morrison, had said at the launching of *A Grain of Truth*, I was a mixture of my mother's sentiment and romance and my father's down-to-earth determination. Paradoxically, the former qualities had encouraged me to retain Honeyneuk on the death of my father, though I knew I would never return to farm it, and the latter had counselled me to sell it in the light of depreciating land values.

It was an agonizing decision, guaranteed to have rattled the rafters of heaven as a point of contention between my parents, but the decision was mine alone and I knew it would have the full support of my mother, who would have accepted the wisdom of realizing my asset, especially when a lack of interest in farming had taken me away from it in the first place.

To distance myself from farming, however, was not to be confused with any lack of feeling for my native Buchan, a passion of love which bit deep into the marrow of my being and had become the quintessence of my soul.

But a Buchan love is an unspeakable one, quiet and dour, bound by native restraint and forced to find an expression in outlets which can run to the bizarre. It remains for me a ruling passion of my blood, a romantic link made the stronger because it has never been capable of fulfilment. An uncaring visitor might tell you that Buchan is a bare, bare place, but nakedness has a charm of its own. To me, she lies with all the allure of a temptress, her beacon head resting on the rocks of Kinnaird, surveying the comely bust which blossoms over Mormond and dips to her navel at Old Deer, before the fair lady spread-eagles herself to the toe-holds of Turriff and Slains, promising, but cool and untouchable.

Those feelings for my native corner of Scotland had to be kept in further check that summer day as I drove in about to Honeyneuk, prepared to meet the folk who would come from far and near for the occasion of my father's roup; for it was much more John Webster's roup than mine. I was the only son who had gone away from it all to the south to make a life of my own, much to the disbelief of my father, who firmly believed that God's handiwork was centred on Buchan and that His world began to go wrong somewhere to the south of Stonehaven, before slithering towards London and into the fiery depths of Hell altogether.

He had spent his entire working life as the Buchan auctioneer, based at Maud, which was a village of only a few hundred people yet could claim to be the biggest weekly cattle market in Britain, the heartland of Aberdeenshire beef. His role as the boss gave him a status to match his expanding girth, and there, with all the fire of good humour and quick temper, he went rollicking along for forty-five years, steeped in the selling of cattle on a Wednesday, measuring land, valuing crops, dispensing sound advice and getting to know the worth of every man and beast within a radius of twenty miles.

But his eye was always on the nearby farm of Honeyneuk and when the laird of Brucklay decided to sell it in 1952, he borrowed every single penny of the purchase price and bought it, moving out with my mother from their council house at 2 Park Crescent, in the village of Maud.

To that furrowed land of Buchan in general, and Honeyneuk in particular, he became wedded as firmly as any man to his wife, a land so sour and grudging those 200 years ago but tamed now and caressed into a fertility which makes it as rich a cattle country as you will find in the kingdom. In so doing, my forebears and their neighbours forged a character that was hard-working, good-humoured, kindly and damnably thrawn.

Their descendants, still sketched by the same sure hand of heredity, came up the Honeyneuk road that day, caught spontaneously by those television cameras which had come to capture a depiction of rural life. Some were encased in motor cars, others came dysting on foot, and there was even the quaint arrival of a figure in shalt and gig, who might have been an Old Testament prophet or a fugitive from the hairy sixties. In fact, he turned out to be David Watson Hood, an artist who had settled at Overhill Smiddy Croft, near my mother's birthplace at Whitehill. His arrival, unplanned and unannounced, came fortuitously to the camera lens to give a weird sense of the continuity which threads itself through the fabric of Scottish rural life.

As those cameras panned across the landscape, I took up the commentary about how the farming life of Buchan had revolved around the village of Maud and particularly its livestock mart, all lying twenty-eight miles to the north of Aberdeen and fourteen miles inland from Peterhead. It was there, in a front room of Fedderate Cottages, that I was born on a July day in the decade of national depression, they say, though to the country child of the thirties it was more of a golden haze of harmony and mellow foxtrots. This was the centre of my universe, bounded by Willie Ogston's smiddy, Lizzie Allan's sweetie shop, the River Ugie and the railway line, Bank's Hill and the Peershoose, Kitchie's Dam and the Creeshie Raa.

Maud Station was the heart and soul of our existence, the junction where the train from Aberdeen split into two sections, one for Fraserburgh (or the Broch, as we knew it) and the other for Peterhead, better known as the Blue Toon. Porters puffing at their Steenhives would dyst along the platform, calling out 'Maud, change for Fraserburgh', and the steam engines would hoot and whistle and thrust themselves into motion, weaving symmetrically outwards from our spacious junction, two halves of a locomotive worm, one heading down through Brucklay, Strichen, Mormond, Lonmay, Rathen and Philorth to the Broch and the other ploughing through the Garden of Buchan by Mintlaw, Longside and Inverugie to Peterhead. This Buchan line had scythed its way through the cornparks of the North-East since 1865, but the infamous Doctor Beeching put an end to all that in the centenary year of 1965, and here, as I strode along the platform that June day of twenty years later, it was hard to believe that such a life had ever existed.

Yet weird images arose before me now to confirm that this had once been much more than a station platform in one small corner of the great railway network of Britain. It was our platform of life, our chance to gaze at the in-coming stranger, to sense the ebb and flow of a throbbing world that lay out yonder.

By this gateway to the rest of the world I had stood as a little boy that September day of 1939, when the Territorials came streaming out of doorways all the way up the village and headed down the Bobby's Brae to join that train to war. Our little station was grand enough to have a John Menzies bookstall, run by Tibby Bruce, who was blind as a bat, and a Refresh which was leased by Lil and Lena Murison. From within that modest hostelry, young men stuffed gill bottles in their pockets and put on a brave face for the adventures ahead. Buchan folk are ill at ease with their emotions, but solid country men and women let slip a tear as that train drew out for a destination unknown, a foray over the neep parks of a foreign land from which many would not return. They steamed out towards Aberdeen, and as I stood there now, re-creating the vision of that September day when war broke out, I could see again their flailing arms, waving from the distance of the Den Wood, and hear their farewell calls, echoing back through the cutting of a line now derelict and overgrown and left behind in the name of progress.

In time, I too had left all this behind and headed off to be a journalist, in Turriff and Aberdeen and then in Glasgow, where you would find me as a sub-editor on the *Daily Express* before branching out as a writer, travelling the world and coming in contact with Prime Ministers and Presidents, interviewing the stars, from Charlie Chaplin, Burt Lancaster, Bing Crosby and Bob Hope to James Mason, Ginger Rogers and Sophia Loren. Not much of that impressed my matter-of-fact father until the day I could tell him that my income had surpassed his own. My spirited mother, warm and understanding, noticed a quiet change of heart, even a pride in the fact that 'the loon's daein nae bad for himsel'.

From the station I wandered along to the mart which had been my father's place of work for more than forty years. Daily day he tramped these floors from which the prime beef of Buchan still finds its way to the top hotels of London. This was his store-cattle ring where, as a boy, he had envied the auctioneer in his rostrum, the central performer in a weekly agricultural drama.

Dad was a crofter's boy from Backhill of Allathan at New Deer, but his father died of an anthrax infection when the boy was eight and there he strove to look after his mother, younger brother and their few beasts, and eventually set out as a drover of cattle to the mart. But his aim was always that auctioneer's box and, in time, he was given the chance to canvass for cattle on his motor bike. By the time I was a child he had graduated to a dickey-backed car with a spare wheel up front and a battery on the running-board.

His ambition achieved, he worked at a dynamic pace with a sense of immortality which amused my mother. 'Ye winna stop for yer ain funeral,' she would chide. But he did. Since 1977 I had carried on his beloved farm, albeit at a great distance and not with the interest and commitment demanded of modern farming. So I made the decision to sell, and there, as I stood in his own rostrum at Maud Mart and heard the echo of his powerful voice, I could not but reflect on the irony that the notice board which had once announced other people's displenish sales had something now to say about John Webster himself.

Just last night, within this very auditorium, the furniture and household effects which had seen my father and mother through their eventful married years, had been put under the hammer of my father's successors. Tomorrow. Tomorrow his implements and most of his cattle would follow suit.

In distant places where folk had furs and jewellery and never fouled a hand in honest toil they had their theatres and opera houses and fanciful entertainments. In a place like Maud they mainly sublimated their dramatic instincts in 'The Roup', an amphitheatre of cut-and-thrust with all the fascination of the chase, the competitive bidding, sometimes to land you with what you wanted and sometimes to make sure Mrs So-and-so didn't get it. Up there in his box my father was the ringmaster, cracking his whip this way and that, teasing, encouraging, cajoling, challenging.

Among the household goods of my childhood, the chanty was always guaranteed to bring some comic relief to the more serious nature of the occasion. 'Come on noo, Mrs Duguid,' my father would rasp out, picking on a lady of vulnerable proportions. 'This should jist aboot fit you!' There would be great guffaws as a willing audience released its imagination on the prospect of one fat lady arranging herself on the limited scope of an enamel chanty. This was Sotheby's with sharn on your boots, a real-life drama for rural folk whose uncompromising life had fashioned them with a steady gait, a kindly heart, an eye for observation and a dry and biting wit.

But the main disposal of John Webster's effects was at Honeyneuk that summer Saturday of 1985, and now that a crowd of 1,000 people had congregated round the tool-shed door, Charlie Morrison, the auctioneer, was calling them to attention to announce the conditions of sale before bursting into that rhythm of rouping in which my father had been the acknowledged expert.

Of smaller build, Charlie Morrison had picked up the art to fine effect, beating out a rataplan of rhetoric which may have been commonplace to the folk of Buchan but was a revelation to the television million, who were captivated by the big tackety boots as they broke into a disco-like accompaniment to the quest for bids. A box of nuts and bolts, with a potential of no more than ten pence, was given as much enthusiasm as a tractor costing thousands. I stood on the perimeter of it all, trying to absorb those elusive nuances of a memorable occasion and casting an eye round the faces, some of my father's generation but others of my own, men grown into the mould of their begetters, with all the skeely tracings of nature, sure and dependable as the night that follows day. Old or young, they came up to tell me what a grand chap my father was, how he had helped them with sound advice over the years. Often enough they were crofter folk, not good with words of gratitude, they said, but maybe I would know what they meant; and they walked away with a silent nod and I knew well and lo'ed them for it.

Those auctioneers who had grown up under the shadow of my father were taking it in turn to preside over a decent dispersal. Norman Law, Ian Emslie, Norman Murison, Charlie Morrison. From the tool-shed door, eident hands kept up the flow of goods for sale, hands that were gnarled from years of work at Honeyneuk. I could not have carried on the farm since my father died had it not been for the two men who worked the place for me. They say the good farm worker is a memory from a bygone age, but that would insult men like Charlie Fraser, my grieve, and Jimmy Mutch, the cattleman.

There was Charlie now at work, surrounded by his three sons, boys in the splendid mould of their father, who would have turned to the land if there had been work for them to do. And there was Jimmy Mutch, who followed his father as the baillie at Honeyneuk and had qualified for the Highland Society's medal for thirty years' service by the time he was forty-nine. It is no condescension to say that these men are the salt of the earth, honest, decent country folk who would put most of us to shame with the effort and integrity which they invest in their daily darg. Another time and my father would have encouraged men of that ilk to become their own masters, such was his belief in the right of the farming folk to benefit from the ownership of their own few acres. Rising costs put that out of the question, and agriculture became the poorer for it; but the downward trend in land prices during the 1980s may well have prefaced a modern revolution in the use of our soil and – who knows? – the small man might well come into his own once more in the new century.

Buchan had always been the working end of Aberdeenshire, championed by that great Parliamentarian Robert Boothby, their MP who happened to be a Conservative but would have been elected no matter his persuasion. Somehow he symbolized that rural culture to which we had belonged for countless generations and from which there was no ready route of exit, even for those of us who had physically separated our daily lives from the tilth of our beginnings.

Disposal of Honeyneuk may have been a sensible decision, but there was no escaping a tug of conscience and a speculation of what John Webster would be making of it this day when 1,000 Buchan folk were milling around his beloved farm in such a gathering as Honeyneuk had never seen. That distant rumbling was a clap of thunder, I hoped, and not the vibration of my father turning in his grave up there in the Kirkyard of Culsh, as a preliminary to stalking down upon this intrusion of his property and scattering them back to their own bit biggings.

Round in the implement shed, Beatrice Cardno, who feeds the farmers on Wednesday mart days, was filling her mince baps and Buchan folk were downing a dram in the warm camaraderie of a country roup. Within their own company, conversation comes easily, free and frank and gloriously good-humoured. I met people like Ian Will, whom I had not seen since the day I left Maud School. Where had we been since those wartime years? Boys grown to men in a world which guarantees little but change; change in our surroundings, no doubt, but change most of all in ourselves.

While Charlie Morrison the auctioneer gyrated on the outside, his namesake, Charlie Morrison the cashier, was gathering in the proceeds of the sale in that old farmhouse of Honeyneuk. All that my father had created in his vision of building a lasting entity of farming was dissolving into liquid cash at the hands of what some would no doubt see as the worthlessness of his wastrel son. When Dad finally accepted that he was not destined for an immortal life, a matter about which he seemed unconvinced for most of his days, he made known that he would like the place carried on. In his heart of hearts I think he knew there would be a limit to that possibility, though he never spoke about it. A blockage of the brain on Burns Night of 1976 put him out of touch with reality in the matter of a minute. He was seventy. He lived for another sixteen months, and I had lingered with the ownership of the farm for another eight years.

But now it was time to turn my back on Honeyneuk, with all its memories and associations, and to hand it over to Jim and Belinda Muir, the kind of hard-working couple of whom my father would have thoroughly approved.

Folk carted away their day's purchases, most of it practical (for Buchan folk are nothing if not practical) but some of it just a souvenir of John Webster; then they came past to say their goodbyes. Now the fields and the byres and the shelves of Honeyneuk lay empty, and an eerie silence was creeping in with the shadows of evening.

How odd that I should speak so much about my father, because, much as I admired him, I was very much closer to my mother, about whom I have said very little. Before I would break this tangible link with Buchan, however, there was one more call to make on that perplexing day. As I have said, my parents lie there in the Kirkyard of Culsh, near the neighbouring village of New Deer, my mother having gone there much too soon for one who so enlivened everything she touched. Through her grandfather, Gavin Greig, she was closely connected to the families of both Robert Burns and Edvard Grieg, whose ancestors went to Norway from Buchan.

It is appropriate that my parents should lie there at Culsh, for they both grew up and lived their entire lives within three miles of that final resting place. The relatives and old neighbours from Maud and New Deer are all there together, including the remains of Gavin Greig and my young cousin, Arthur Argo. From such a place of peace I can gaze out over the Buchan landscape and conjure up pictures of a childhood that pulsated with love and laughter, hard work and good fellowship. When the furrows of spring had produced the corn of late summer, the stubble of autumn and the joyous cry of 'Winter!' when the last sheaf had been forked, it was time for the meal-an'-ale and the bothy ballads.

But my mother's horizons stretched far beyond the cornfields of Buchan. From her wireless, she was just as much at home with *The Sleeping Beauty* of Tchaikovsky as with *The Barnyards of Delgaty*. Among her favourite pieces of music was

Dvořák's 'New World' Symphony. 'I want it played at my funeral,' she used to joke. 'Tell Johnny Walker, the organist.' So we did. And the strains of 'Goin' Home' from that Dvořák symphony followed her up the brae to Culsh, strains which linger with me even at a time when I have cut my ties with Honeyneuk and seek out this very special panorama from the heights of the kirkyard. From here, by the Monument of Culsh, I can see Mains of Whitehill, where she was born, and the route she had taken to the school at New Deer. Down the brae to Maud, just two miles away, she had gone to spend her entire married life, in the village itself and later at Honeyneuk.

As the day draws to its close, I can just see the sombre outline of the farm steading, brooding in the last of the evening light. All around me is peace and contentment. In spite of the perplexities of the day, there is a sense of embracing the world in one wide sweep, suddenly identifying its multifarious elements in a pattern that begins to make some kind of sense. In microcosm, I suppose, that wider world is represented here within the landscape spread now before me. As that Dvořák symphony swells once more in haunting harmony and I stand here alone in soliloquy, I must surely know now, if I didn't know it before, that I am a Buchan man for ever.

CHAPTER THREE

—•◦•—

Champagne Breakfast

On the morning of my fiftieth birthday I had wandered along to Fedderate Cottages, in the village of Maud, and presented myself at the door of Bill and Isobel Clark, who had been well forewarned of my mission.

I had come, complete with bottle of champagne, for the sentimental ritual of standing in the small front room where, exactly half a century earlier, I had been born at a quarter to nine on a Wednesday morning, an event of such insignificance that my father could not have been expected to disturb his weekly routine of selling cattle at the local mart.

For Wednesday was the big day of the week in Maud (some might say the only day of the week in Maud), and John Webster was the central figure in that conglomeration of cattle, sheep and pigs being bought and sold in front of a couthy congregation of Aberdeenshire farmers, who brought with them to the village thoroughfares all the dysting gait of the plough-rig and the warm aroma of the Bogie Roll which came yoaming from their Steenhive pipes to mingle with cattle breath and turn the atmosphere of the sale-ring into a steaming, blue-grey concoction.

News of my birth that morning in 1931 was carried to the edge of the auctioneer's rostrum by a neighbour's daughter, little Elma Craig, and my father paused just long enough to absorb my grandmother's note before proceeding with the sale of the next bit sharny-hipped heifer.

Fifty years later, it happened to be a Wednesday once again and down the village streets came the corresponding parade of Buchan cattle, driven by the sons and grandsons of that earlier generation, creating an illusion that very little had changed in the intervening period, and indeed, in the more subtle areas of our existence, maybe very little had.

At a quarter to nine I stood four-square by the corner of the room where my mother had undergone the agonies of childbirth, before being rushed off to the City Hospital in Aberdeen (where she had once been a trainee nurse) and left at the end of the ward, in an expectation of the early death which came almost invariably to sufferers of peritonitis in those distant days.

Gritting her teeth in a determination to return to the newborn child, she drew back from death's door after weeks on the threshold, and the surgeon came to see us many years later, still marvelling at the will power which alone had pulled her through.

So there was no doubt about the subject of a silent toast as friends dropped in to share a glass of champagne that Wednesday morning and to exchange stories from our village life of fifty years before.

When the ritual was over, I stood at that cottage door and mused over the mileage I had covered since first I ventured down the steps of Fedderate Cottages, the bank of experience I had built up, the people and the places, the joys and the heartaches.

I had come back to my very first reference point of existence, to the room where I had gasped the first burst of air, peered out at the opening glimmer of God's light and taken those first faltering steps on the journey of the unknown.

On that same day fifty years earlier, according to the local daily newspaper, the Aberdeen *Press and Journal*, King George V was holding a glittering reception at the Palace of Holyroodhouse; Oswald Mosley was leading his New Party of five into the Commons, to the jeers of the ruling Socialists from whom he had just broken away; the weather forecast was predictably middling; and Raggie Morrison's shop in St Nicholas Street, Aberdeen, was selling leatherette coats at 6s 6d (thirty-two and a half pence).

In Aberdeen, the famous comedian Tommy Lorne was appearing at His Majesty's Theatre, the mysterious Doctor Walford Bodie from Macduff was performing his electrical feats at the Tivoli and the inimitable Harry Gordon was starring at his Beach Pavilion, with Flanagan and Allen among his supporting acts.

On the National Radio programme, Henry Hall's Gleneagles Band was playing from 11 p.m. till midnight and the *Press and Journal* gave highlights of twenty-nine foreign stations, from a Beethoven concert on Algiers Radio to the waltzes of Vienna Radio.

Nearer home there were more mundane matters like hoeing matches at Lumphanan, Monymusk and Vale of Alford and a bowling match at Maud, where the local rink of Hector Macphail, Hector Mavor, J. G. Morrison and James Murray were beating the Causewayend Old Boys of Aberdeen.

If that decade of the thirties had ushered in a national depression then the folk of Maud would be less affected than most, for they had long survived on a staple diet of meal, milk and tatties and were perhaps no better or worse off than they had ever been.

Material hardship and deprivation had long been the accepted lot in this cold shoulder of Scotland, the land of Buchan which cut inland from the Moray Firth by the holy place of Gardenstown, down through Turriff and round by Methlick to Ellon and eastward to the great North Sea.

Whereas the Lord in His infinite mercy had given lush land to those who languished in places like the Lothians and down through the English countryside, he proposed a stiffer examination of character for his Pictish peasantry in that North-East corner of Scotland called Buchan.

Not for them the soft meadows of the south, the willing tilth that surrenders to the first hint of proposition from a ploughshare with all the haste of a whore.

Instead, there was bog and whin and peaty moss, moraines of long stony ridge and barren hill, defying all but the sternest effort of mankind's best specimens to wrest it from sour intransigence and turn it into something that might pass for cultivation. The folk who have farmed that land of Buchan since the time of Prince Charlie have created their own living monument to the limits of human endurance, the fortitude of ordinary men and women challenged to a survival that might have seemed of such dubious nature as to make it hardly worth the effort.

That monument is writ large, not on slabs of granite but in mile after mile of fertile field, barley and oats, turnip and potatoes, the rich green of pasture and, in this late twentieth century, the mustard yellow that might once have been taken for the weed of skelloch but is now the profitable crop of oilseed rape.

The epitaph to generations of hardy Buchan folk who broke their backs and maybe their spirits is there in the black and white of well-fed cattle, in the neat trim of drysteen dykes and the undersoil network of drainage.

My own forefathers were of that breed, not least Grandpa Barron, my mother's father, who made his own contribution to the improvement of the land, once he became the tenant farmer at Mains of Whitehill, but who could recall the customary discomfort and health hazards of the halflin, which he suffered in the last quarter of the nineteenth century, when he slept in an open bothy above the horse-stalls.

Grandpa Barron would wander across the brae to the farm of Atherb for a news with a man for whom he had the keenest admiration. John Milne was not only an improving farmer but a man who so sensed the historic significance of the great agricultural romance which had been enacted without due recognition of its miraculous proportions, that he made some effort to put it down on paper.

At the turn of the present century, John Milne could give my grandfather a first-hand account of his own grand-uncle in the eighteenth century, who was the goadsman of a ten-owsen plough on the farmlands by Maud, as well as being obliged to thresh the corn crop by flail (a murderous task) for the princely wage of twenty-five shillings, or £1.25 today, per half year!

They wore home-made brogues but just as often went barefooted, even to church, where they would put on their socks and shoes before entering and take them off again when they came out. In those days they made up for a scarcity of food for cattle and horses by crushing whins with a heavy wooden hammer; for their own diet they concocted a dish which Grandpa Barron still enjoyed until his death on New Year's Day of 1948. That was the old-fashioned offering of sowens, made of oat husks and fine meal, steeped and strained and fermented to a solid mass which was eaten like porridge.

That and piz-meal brose were two doubtful delicacies to which he failed to convert me in my childhood days, though I willingly joined in the ritual of 'milk-an'-breid', which amounted to a bowl of milk, into which a corter of oatcakes was broken and supped in hearty spoonfuls by young men who wanted to grow up with mush on their arms.

John Milne's father took on a lease at Atherb in 1836 and embarked on the kind of bare existence which makes you realize that, whatever the hardships and injustices of today, we have much to appreciate when set against the trials of those ancestors who slaved last century. This is the kind of memory John Milne was leaving to people like my grandfather:

> I can remember my father and mother taking but one cup of tea, and that only in the morning, sweetening it with treacle because that was cheaper than sugar. The children got no tea excepting one cup on the Sabbath morning, while tobacco was a luxury not to be thought of.
>
> Being the only boy, I had to work as soon as I was able – and indeed before I was able – and 'tis with sadness that I look back on those early days. My education was curtailed and interrupted . . . and even when at school in winter, I had to work morning and evening, plying the flail when I should have been at lessons. My father began his improvement by draining the bogs with stone drains. Part of my first work was to fill the stones into a barrow when the ground was too soft to carry carts, or to hand them to my father as he built the drains. During the lease, we put in about 4,000 yards of those stone drains.

The boulder stones which were later to plague my own father on the neighbouring farm of Honeyneuk were an even greater hazard at Atherb a century earlier.

> We began to take out the boulders [said John Milne], and this was the heaviest and most fatiguing work of all. We had no mechanical appliances except long levers and blocks. They were hard to bore for blasting. Four or five feet was all a man could do in a day. Many a time have I set up a box barrow to shelter me from the drifting snow or the sleety shower and drilled a hole. Once we got them loose and free from earth all round, we put on a fire which broke them up. Bluestone splits readily when exposed to heat. In winter the boulders were dirty and wore the skin off our hands. Often after a hard day's work among these stones, with tired muscles and aching hands, I have been unable to enjoy refreshing sleep at night, but in a feverish dream repeated the work of the day.

That farm of Atherb had further intrigued my grandfather because it was where they had dug up a cairn known as 'The Fear'd Place', for the purpose of making a road, and found large quantities of human bones and flint arrowheads. The bones were mixed with charred oak and covered to a depth of three feet by stones showing signs of having been subjected to heat. There were circular and semi-circular cavities nearby. Whether it was a mass burial ground from some long-forgotten battle or the remains of a fort, with the occupants burned out by their enemies, will remain for ever a mystery.

So much for the recollections of a Buchan loon in the mid-rig of the last century, a time when the name of Maud would hardly have been known. There was just the hamlet of Bank, called after the farm of Bank of Behitch, where horse-carriers between Aberdeen and the lesser towns of Peterhead and Fraserburgh would unhitch their animals for food and rest at the parting of the ways. The name of Behitch had nothing to do with the unhitching of the horses but merely meant the Bank of the Birch Tree.

That Y-shaped route between the three North-East towns became further emphasized in the middle of last century by the building of the Buchan and Formartin railway line when, once again, the village now known as Maud was to be the parting of the ways for the Aberdeen train as it split into two halves, which wended their separate ways to Peterhead and Fraserburgh.

With such a junction springing up around 1865, the original village of Bank, situated in the parish of Old Deer, was destined to spread over the Old Maud Burn and into the adjoining parish of New Deer to form a larger village, which came to be known as New Maud.

The convenience of the railway turned it into a natural meeting point for district councillors and Presbyterian parsons alike, and in 1866 the twenty-four parishes of the area pooled their resources to build the Buchan Combination Poor's House, still standing today as Maud Hospital.

So a place of 200 or 300 people began to cluster round that railway junction, and in time it grew to more than 700 inhabitants and to have three butchers, three bakers, four grocers, two shoemakers, two watchmakers, joiners, millwrights, cabinetmakers, a saddler, a druggist, dressmakers and a corn merchant, not to mention a Post Office, two hotels, a station refreshment room and Lizzie Allan's sweetie shop. The village sloped downwards past the station to the old Bank Village, which nestled at the foot of Bank's Hill and contains to this day the kirk and the hospital and a single streetful of douce dwellings.

CHAPTER FOUR

---•◦•---

Roar Like a Dove

Having travelled around the world in my years as a journalist, I have paused at many an unlikely corner between Honeyneuk and Hong Kong, Maud and Moscow, and wondered what prompted enough people in that particular location to find a reason for permanent settlement. Why not closer to the amenities of a city or the warmth of a more hospitable climate?

No doubt there are people who have chanced upon my native land of Buchan and asked themselves the self-same question. So perhaps I have been able to answer my own queries by the same token as I can give a convincing answer to theirs.

It takes only a minor catalytic agent to spark off the spirit of community, just a few people with a common cause, like that cluster which gave rise to the village of New Maud in the middle of the last century. Soon the convenience of the railway commended itself to the agricultural needs of the Buchan area. Where better to build the livestock marts from which the animals could then fan out across the North-East of Scotland and even further to the butchers of the south, finding their way to the tables of the grand hotels in London?

But even without the special circumstances of central convenience, there would still have been a spirit of community, just as there is in other parts of the rural scene not so blessed with amenity. For the people who live by the loneliness of the land develop a sense of responsibility for it, becoming as thirled to its tilth as they are to the flesh and blood of their own breeding.

In the sparseness of population the folk become responsible for one another, dependent on each other, not with an ostentatious display of caring but in a quiet observance of unobtrusive decencies.

From the stability of a rural setting it is not too hard to pick up the strands of ancestry and to gain some sense of the patterns of living which your forefathers were managing to create. You can easily imagine how the surrounding farmers of Clackriach and Atherb and Honeyneuk and Affleck gathered together one night about 1825 and decided to raise enough money to provide a local school, in the shape of a little thackit hoosie, down by the hamlet of Bank. Up at the farm of Honeyneuk, which was later to become my own home, the education of girls was undertaken in a room of the old farmhouse, it seems, by the farmer's daughter, Miss Paterson.

In the second half of the century, they were schooling the boys down the brae at Bank village, in what later became the Masonic Lodge, while the girls were now being educated at the other end of Maud, in what was to become Willie Ogston's smiddy to a later generation.

In 1896 they combined these two inadequate establishments and built a new central school by the picturesque avenue which looks down across the station to the hospital and the kirk and then upwards to the knoll of Bank's Hill with its clump of trees atop.

My great-grandfather, Gavin Greig, the playwright, composer and folk-song collector, was present on that opening day of April, 1896, and it was to that same building exactly forty years later (the Aberdeenshire school year started in April then) that I was led by my mother for my first day at Maud Higher Grade School. The original headmaster, John Law, still lived by the playground wall, as did one of his first teachers, Miss Slessor. One of my primary teachers in those innocent days was none other than Bell Duncan, who had been a pupil at that girls' school in the smiddy away back in 1888 and could bring us the warm reassurance of a life that endured with surprising stability, considering we were now on the other side of that great divide, the First World War, which separated the old order from the new.

In Bell Duncan's schooldays the spiritual life of the village had blossomed from an early mission to a proper *quoad sacra* parish church, which gained for its first minister a former

33

Donside ploughman, William Cowie, who was to seed a highly talented family. Bell Duncan and her sister Jessie became close friends with Mr Cowie's daughters, one of whom was to emerge as a great British playwright of the twentieth century, under her pen-name of Lesley Storm.

With her real name of Mabel Cowie, she graduated at Aberdeen University in the early 1920s and first attracted public attention with novels like *Head in the Wind*, *Small Rain* and *Strange Man's Home*, which shocked the more pious of her father's flock: She married a Dr Clark, who practised from the highly fashionable London address of 25 South Terrace, Kensington, and it was there, on my first visit to the big city in 1950, that I ventured along, knocked at her door and introduced myself as a loon fae Maud. (I can now marvel at the effrontery of it!)

Lesley Storm took me in and entertained me for the afternoon, a delightful hostess, still recognizable as a bonny lassie from Maud but now with the overtones of sophistication that had come with living among the literati of London and being dined and wined by men like Lord Beaverbrook, who was among her greatest admirers. (He included her picture on the front page when he produced his very first edition of the *Scottish Daily Express* in 1928.)

She recalled with affection her childhood in Maud, the school, the people, the pranks, the boy-friends, the Forces who had passed by during the First World War. When she asked what I had been doing in London, I told her of a splendid film I had seen the previous evening. It was called *Tony Draws a Horse*, a humorous psychological film about a boy who, when asked at school to draw a horse, gave exaggerated embellishments to its most potent anatomical features! She smiled at me warmly. 'I wrote that story in 1939,' she said.

Lesley Storm had also written the screenplay of Graham Greene's *The Fallen Idol* and was on the point of giving us some of her own finest masterpieces, plays like *Black Chiffon*, *The Day's Mischief*, *Roar Like a Dove* and *Time and Yellow Roses*. From the film rights of just three of her plays she had earned £150,000, a sizeable sum in any age but a fortune in the 1950s.

Once I had established myself in journalism, many years later, I was able to meet her again and to interview her for none other than Lord Beaverbrook's *Daily Express*. She also returned to Maud in 1961 to visit her old friends, the Miss Duncans, while *Time and Yellow Roses* was having its world première at His Majesty's Theatre in Aberdeen.

But the reputation for laying the foundations of notable citizens was not confined to Mr Cowie, who remained as minister at Maud for thirty-five years. Round the hill, at the farm of Mains of Clackriach, one of the workers had a daughter, Jean Minty, who grew up to be the mother of Lady Isabel Barnett, distinguished as a television personality in programmes like *What's My Line*, alongside the memorable Gilbert Harding. Young Isabel used to come back to Buchan, where her favourite playmate was Mona Low, now Mrs Dawson of Coronation Cottages, Maud.

Further down the road, at the Aden Estate by Old Deer, Colonel Russell was rearing a daughter who was to become the mother of Lord Whitelaw, the familiar Willie Whitelaw of Mrs Thatcher's governments.

CHAPTER FIVE

Like Robbie Burns

That panorama of local history had passed vividly before my eyes that July morning of my fiftieth birthday as I stood at the doorway of Fedderate Cottages, Maud, and tried to encompass the half century that had flitted by since first I saw light in what was then a but-and-ben.

My parents had begun their married life more modestly in a rat-infested hovel at Mill of Bruxie, two miles from Maud, where my father stood guard by the cottage door, firing off his double-barrel gun at the invading vermin. My mother was already pregnant, but before the birth of their only child they would move into the village, to the greater comfort of Fedderate Cottages, a stone-and-lime block of eight flats between Kitchie's Dam and the school, which would seem like Paradise after Bruxie, even if it was not yet blessed with inside toilets.

And there, as I stood by the doorway of my birth, I had clear recollections of living there, though we had moved to a council house at 2 Park Crescent, less than a hundred yards away, by the time I was three years and four months old.

Now I was striving to separate the fact from childhood fantasy and to flesh out the skeleton of memory which had followed me through the 1930s into the dark excitement of the Second World War and out again to the bleakness of a post-war youth.

So many changes and so many different standpoints, bewildering enough in themselves without nature's own hazardous journey from boy to man. How much is ever real?

Well, for a start, I remember that flitting of November, 1934, when I was three, in which I was entrusted with the task of carrying the biscuit tins from Fedderate Cottages up the back lane and past the midden to Park Crescent. Neighbours like John Craig and Jimmy Pyper helped my father to carry the furniture. Around that same time, I recall my aunt's wedding in the village hall at the neighbouring New Pitsligo. Even before that, I have vague impressions of two local lads, Charlie Hunter and my mother's favourite message-boy, Sandy Dyer, a chubby rascal in freckles, dirding my pram round Fedderate Cottages as part of their lorry-driving fantasies, all the while terrorizing the infant into bewildered silence.

In that decade of the thirties I can trace a pattern of awakening to the joys and excitements of a big wide world: the feein markets, when farm servants were engaged for the term; the skirl of the recruiting pipe bands for those who didn't find a fee; the general tenor of a rural way of life with its sights and sounds and scents.

I can still hear the mellow saxophones of Roy Fox and Lew Stone on the national wireless, the gloom of King George V's funeral and the stir of Abdication for his son, the Prince of Wales, which had us riveted round the sets for a sombre speech of which I had only the vaguest understanding.

It was in that year of the old king's death that I was welcomed into the fold of Maud School by the kindly Miss Catto, who had come from her native Aberdeen in the year of the General Strike, a decade earlier. What a different world it had seemed that April day of 1936 when a tearful mother delivered me unwillingly into the care of the infant class. With a motherly manner, the golden-haired Miss Catto had set us down to a routine of slates and plasticine and counting beads, in front of a roaring fire enclosed by a sturdy guard-rail.

In that warm and happy atmosphere the foundations of life were well and truly laid, the Three Rs of reading, writing and 'rithmetic well and truly taught, and, if the truth be known, the first flickerings of love well and truly stirred. Across the passage sat Doris Symon, dark ringlets dangling against her lily-white skin, so clean and neat and gently perfumed, fine-boned and truly beautiful. Prompted surely by nature, we would reach out a touching hand and blush in the bewilderment of alien forces. Ah, for the tingling beauty of innocence!

Innocent, too, we were of that Depression which must have

been raging outby in the thirties, though it did not seem to intrude overmuch on our rural life with its hot summers and dramatic winters (or so they seemed) which blocked us in for weeks on end and turned the Christmas card of the artist's brush into a picturesque reality.

The North-East childhood of the 1930s seemed as smooth and golden as Miss Catto's hair, uncomplicated by the gathering troubles of an outside world, the insanity of which was conveyed to us by means of the wireless (but then only if Bob Sangster had charged your wet batteries). Up and beyond Bank's Hill lay the foreign lands that folk spoke about; but our little universe was safe in the folding arms of the River Ugie as it flowed down from Bonnykelly, past Brucklay and Honeyneuk on the way to Old Deer and the North Sea beyond; safely defined it was by the railway lines which curled around our perimeter.

Within the limits of that universe we knew contentment and excitement in agreeable proportions, the hard work of country folk still lightened by an active and home-made social relief. With Aikey Fair and the feein markets came the hawkers and pedlars, selling preens, pints and bars of soap, fish-wives from the Broch bearing heavy creels on their backs; the visiting circuses of Dick's and Pinder's, modest enough when you look back but major events in their time. Among those pedlars was old Geordie Robertson, whose mathematics were simple. When my grandmother remonstrated with him about the price of a small item, he had a ready answer: 'Na na, Mrs Barron, I buy them for a penny and sell them for tippence – just one per cent profit, ye see.'

There was croquet and crumpets, and the unforgettable waft of hot cheese-cakes from the fresh ovens of Morrison's Bakery. Not the least of it was the excitement of the yellow van appearing round the Hill o' Clackriach from Peterhead to herald the arrival of Luigi Zanre, who made the finest ice-cream in all Christendom. But more of Luigi later.

In front of a roaring fire in the infant classroom, Miss Catto served lunchtime cocoa for country bairns who had brought their 'piece' in a bag, and she rounded off a perfect week with her Friday afternoon caramel. So she fed the bodies and nurtured the child mind with the basics of a sound education. By the time we moved up school from Miss Catto to Miss Duncan and Miss Morrison we were already benefiting from a thorough grounding. For amusement, I still keep my dictation book of 1938, from which I discover that 'A little mouse has made its home within my house' and 'The pilot had a leather coat, also goggles' at the Croydon Aerodrome which was the focal point of all flying interest in those early days of Biggles.

Those thoughts of Maud School were revolving freely in my head on that anniversary visit when I was striding out towards a rendezvous with two very special ladies. There they were, coming towards me, just as they had crossed the playground at Maud all those years ago – none other than Miss Catto and Miss Morrison, looking little different from the impressions I had guarded for nearly half a century. Miss Catto was the senior by quite a number of years, having taught at Maud from 1926 until 1942, but happily she survives in good health into 1987, living at Seafield Gardens, Aberdeen. Miss Morrison is an active citizen of Banchory, where she is now Mrs Reith of Glassel Road. Having arrived at Maud in 1939, she remained throughout the war years before moving to Kittybrewster School in Aberdeen, which was to count among its former pupils such diverse talents as Denis Law, the footballer, and Lord Armstrong, former Head of the Civil Service and Chairman of the Midland Bank.

So we chatted over old times and rekindled the sense of a bygone age which had slipped so quickly and elusively out of our reach. As time creeps upon us, quiet and unnoticed, the mundane things of life which seem scarcely to merit a mention take on the gloss of history.

We remembered a rural enclosure of contented people, unconcerned with class or creed and forging for themselves a steady rhythm of honest toil and simple pleasure which produced a happiness beyond analysis. We remembered the names and the faces, the laughter in the still country air, and the dreaded scourge of consumption and diphtheria which regularly stalked our village classrooms to bear away another innocent child in the sorrow of a little white coffin.

Miss Catto remembered that I had stated an ambition to be 'jist like Robbie Burns' and that she had re-told it in the staffroom, expressing the hope that I would not become too much like Robbie Burns!

We remembered the new arrival in the infant room, a farm boy who sat all day just gazing up at the ventilation grille in the ceiling. At the end of the day he affected an adult posture and asked the teacher 'Are ye ill wi rottens?' which, translated into English, means 'Are you troubled with rats?' The boy, who grew up to be a solid farmer, was clearly more concerned with rodent infestation than primary education.

There was also Miss Duncan's story about the day she was giving a lesson on children's pets when one boy announced that his dog was called 'Moreover'. When she expressed doubts about such a name, the little chap assured her of his authority: 'Ay Miss, it says it in the Bible. "Moreover the dog came and licked his sores."'

Imagine the chagrin of discovering that, in the 1930s, these noble ladies were being rewarded with the princely salary of £180 a year if they were graduates and £130 if they were not. Out of that came 18s. a week (ninety pence) which they paid for digs to Ma Smith at Woodville, not to mention those caramels and assorted sundries which came out of their own pockets without thought of recompense.

Their multifarious duties included the unpaid care and collection of our pennies for that same Aberdeen Savings Bank account which, in 1986, gave me preferential treatment for buying shares in the flotation of the TSB! But the service of such ladies could not be measured in pounds, shillings and pence. Their contribution to human happiness and well-being, helping people to make the most of what they were given, is reflected in the lives of their former pupils, countless hundreds who have gone forth into a busy world, cautious and respectful to a fault, only to find to their surprise that the primary grounding in schools like Maud had already fitted them for comparison with more senior levels elsewhere.

It does not surprise me to learn now that students of such matters have come to the conclusion that, during the last century at least, the North-East was the best educated part of Scotland and had the highest literacy rate in all Britain.

That has been the achievement and the reward of all the Miss Cattos and Miss Morrisons and Miss Duncans who have graced our Scottish schools down the years.

CHAPTER SIX

Greig and Grieg

I have never been impressed by, nor even fully understood, the notion of the 'old-established family', since it must surely follow from the plain facts of life that all families stretch back to the same kind of genesis, whether you believe in the phenomenon of Adam and Eve or not.

But the likelihood that we are all much of an age does not occlude the fact that there are branches and twigs of the old hereditary oak which produce much more colour than others. At my grandmother's knee I was given an early lesson on how there came to be a touch of blossom in the forestry of my own family, not through any sense of braggadocio but by the simple duty of passing on the story.

On three sides of my grandparentage, the Websters, Watsons and Barrons, we were fairly plain and predictable country folk, striving to make two corns grow where one grew before and plodding our way through the various travails that beset the Scottish peasantry those few generations ago. Even the fourth strand of the grandparent base, the Greigs, began in similar fashion in the Fraserburgh district, towards Rathen, Lonmay and Cairnbulg, but the even tenor of that heredity was somewhat diverted by the injection of less mundane elements.

For a start, those Greigs claimed earlier cousinship with the Alexander Greig who left Mosstown of Cairnbulg in 1770 to settle in Bergen, where he became the great-grandfather of Edvard Grieg, national composer of Norway and one of the most creative talents in musical history.

Whatever the closeness of the family link, there was certainly a strong resemblance between Edvard Grieg and a corresponding member of the Greig family who stayed in Scotland – Gavin Greig, who not only looked like his 'distant cousin' but had

developed a powerful talent for music, to the point that he too
became a composer, brilliant organist, poet and playwright, but
known best of all perhaps for his famous collection of folk
songs, claimed by those who know about such matters to be
the best of its kind in the world.

All of that, incidentally, was achieved while he pursued his
bread-and-butter occupation as headmaster of a rural school in
the Buchan district of Aberdeenshire. By coincidence, however,
the person of Gavin Greig was further enhanced by a more
clear-cut relationship, which arrived through his mother, Mary
Moir, who came directly from the same Burness family, near
Stonehaven, which produced Robert Burns, the National Bard
of Scotland.

Gavin Greig himself was brought up at Parkhill of Dyce (not
far from the present Aberdeen Airport), where his father was
forester on the estate. I have said much about him in my earlier
book, *A Grain of Truth*, so for the moment let me condense
him to being the classic example of a Scottish lad o' pairts,
graduating from Aberdeen University and settling at Whitehill
of New Deer, where he became headmaster at the age of
twenty-two. There he began to father his nine children, the
eldest of whom was Edith, the same grandmother who was
telling me this story at her knee in the 1930s.

The route of those Greigs who left the shores of Buchan for
the fjords of Norway, however, needs further explanation. With
the long-standing links between Scotland and Scandinavia, it
was not surprising that a certain Mr Wallace from Banff became
the British Consul in Bergen. He happened to be a friend of the
Greig family from Mosstown of Cairnbulg and it was to work
in Mr Wallace's office that Alexander Greig left home in 1770,
at the age of thirty-one.

He settled so well in that role that he eventually succeeded Mr
Wallace as British Consul, while never surrendering one whit of
his Scottishness. Twice a year, in fact, he used to cross the North
Sea in a little boat just to attend communion in the kirk back
home! By the time he was followed in the Consul's job by his son
and grandson, they had conformed to the continental style of

spelling and transposed the vowels to turn Greig into Grieg.

None of that would have gained much attention, and indeed the North-East of Scotland might have bothered very little about claiming their origins, had it not been for the genius who turned up in the next generation. Edvard Grieg, born in Bergen in 1843, was soon establishing himself as one of the greatest living composers, bringing the mountains and fjords alive with the power and passion of his music.

His compositions for Ibsen's *Peer Gynt* and the Piano Concerto in A Minor were just two of the creations in an illustrious career which brought him into contact with everyone from Liszt to Hans Christian Andersen. Significantly perhaps, the intense awareness of the folk heritage was a prime characteristic of Edvard Grieg, just as it was in his distant relative in Scotland, Gavin Greig, who was born just thirteen years after the composer.

The two men never met, but my grandmother did remember her father leaving home one day on a long journey to hear Edvard Grieg giving a piano recital. She thought he went to Edinburgh; but being of such a retiring nature, he apparently did not go backstage to introduce himself. Some have expressed doubts about Grieg ever having visited Scotland, on the grounds that he was a very bad sailor, but the man himself put the record straight in a remarkable conversation which is recorded by the late John Cranna, former harbour treasurer of Fraserburgh, who undertook a great deal of research in these matters of local history. Cranna told us about a Morayshire minister, the Rev. W. A. Gray, who was visiting Norway and who gave this account of the surprise which came upon him in a Laerdal hotel:

> Scarcely had I taken my place in the hotel porch after supper for a smoke in the cool night air when Grieg stood beside me alone and lit his cigar. His figure was even shorter and slighter than I first imagined it to be.
>
> Everyone speaks to everyone in a Norwegian hotel. I accosted him, introducing myself briefly and any doubt I had as to the character of my reception was at once set at

rest. Off went the hat with a courteous Scandinavian sweep; the clear blue eyes glanced keenly into my face; the attitude was of frank and friendly attention. The talk (Grieg speaks fluent English, only now and again interjecting a Norsk word) turned first upon Scotland. The musician asked in what part of Scotland I lived and I answered 'Not very far from the home of your forefathers.'

'Then,' said Herr Grieg, 'you live near Fraserburgh. Alexander Greig, my great-grandfather, who afterwards changed his name to Grieg, emigrated from Fraserburgh last century. See,' he said, displaying the seal at the end of his watch chain, with the figure of a ship among stormy waves, and the motto *Ad spes infracta*, 'here is our crest; it is the same as that of the Scottish Greigs. Yes,' he continued, 'I have various ties in Scotland. I have Scottish friends; my godmother was Scottish – Mrs Stirling; she lived near the town of the same name. I know something of your Scottish writers too, especially Carlyle. I am fond of reading Carlyle; in what part of Scotland was he born? And I admire Edinburgh – Princes Street, the gardens, the old town, the castle – ah, they are beautiful, beautiful. Edinburgh people are very kind.

'They have asked me repeatedly to visit them and to play and I would do so willingly if it were not for the sea. I am the very worst of sailors. Once, some years ago, I crossed from Bergen to Aberdeen. I shall never forget that night of horrors, never!'

We turned to the subject of Scottish music. 'I admire it greatly,' said Herr Grieg, 'and I find a similarity between your Scottish melodies and our Norwegian ones, especially when the sentiment is – what do you call it – *alvorlig*, grave, serious.'

The Reverend Mr Gray did well with his near-verbatim account of a rare meeting, giving some hint of what a marvellous occasion it would have been if only Gavin Greig and Edvard Grieg had found each other's company.

CHAPTER SEVEN

On Mormond Hill

From Granny Barron I gained a perspective of our family history, brought alive by first-hand tales from the last century; tales like the visits of that greatest of fiddlers, J. Scott Skinner, King of Strathspey, to the family home at the Schoolhouse of Whitehill, where he and Gavin Greig cemented their friendship and collaborated in musical works, not least the famous *Harp and Claymore* volume.

Gavin Greig, a tall, lean, scholarly man whose name brought light to the eyes of those who remembered him, had become one of the most loved and revered of the North-East sons, as far away as the academic cloisters of Edinburgh and even on the continent, where they found it hard to understand why a man of such international calibre should closet himself in what seemed to them the backwater of rural Aberdeenshire.

But that was where he belonged and where he was at his happiest, a brilliant conversationalist as naturally and uncondescendingly at ease with the farm servants of his beloved Buchan as with the erudite professors who came to seek him out from distant parts. They were all the same to him.

As a child I knew little about his novels, which were often published in the serialized fashion of the last century (*Logie o' Buchan* was re-published by Bisset's of Aberdeen in 1986). But I was well aware of his musical plays, like *Mains's Wooin'* and *Mains Again*, which have remained in production for nearly a century, from that opening night at New Deer in 1894, when the leading lady was the Buchan beauty of her day, Nellie Metcalfe, who later married the well-known local farmer, athlete and writer Archie Campbell of Auchmunziel, by whom she bore that distinguished Scottish poetess of modern times, Flora Garry.

So I would be taken to productions of those Doric classics in town and village halls around the country and, in the fullness of adulthood, would find myself invited to say a few words, as the great-grandson of the author.

I became deeply aware, too, of his presidential part in a rather special body of people, the Buchan Field Club, a collection of the best brains in the North-East of Scotland who met for the purpose of studying the natural sciences, archaeology, history and literature of Buchan and to interest the young in such studies. Happily, the public interest in that local background, which was strong in Gavin Greig's day, is stronger again in the last quarter of the twentieth century than it was in the middle portion, with the activities of the Buchan Field Club extended by a Buchan Heritage Society.

There is now an annual festival of local speech and music and a splendid heritage centre at Lord Whitelaw's ancestral home of Aden, by Old Deer, where my father's old harvest binder from Honeyneuk has been among the latest exhibits of traditional hardware, still in use for the cutting of oats.

While public speaking has never been a strength of mine, I was nevertheless prevailed upon to address the Buchan Field Club at the annual dinner in Strichen in 1983, held in the same Freemasons' Hotel where they used to meet in the days of Gavin Greig. Such an engagement compelled me to some rewarding research before facing so distinguished a gathering and the results enabled me to place my own lifetime more securely into the context of local history.

This is a summary of what I said at Strichen that night, with some embellishments from what I had intended to say:

On an August day of 1904, this very club gathered here in the village of Strichen and went on an excursion up Mormond Hill, under the leadership of my great-grandfather, Gavin Greig, who was even then on the way to fame as a playwright and composer but more so as the man who collected the folk songs of the North-East. He had to travel only from the Schoolhouse of Whitehill, a few miles from here, but others that day came from as far as London and Kent. They assembled on the arrival of the afternoon train and drove up the hill as far as Brans Farm and thereafter the ascent was accomplished on foot. They visited the Resting Cairns, the Hunt Stone, Rob Gibb's Lodge, the White Horse and the Deer.

Having enjoyed the view from the summit and cast their eyes over Buchan, they descended to hold a meeting in the Freemasons' Hotel where we sit now. After speeches a good deal more scholarly than you are going to hear now, the company sat down to an excellent tea, purveyed by Mrs Mackay.

In a world which seems to change at a bewildering rate, it may be difficult for us in the 1980s to imagine what it was like all those years ago. It is a common fault to believe that the people were stiff and quaint and not so alert as ourselves, but a glance at the quality of address produced in your own transactions shows how scholarly and perceptive and humorous they really were in those days.

As a preliminary to coming here tonight I did not engage in the worthwhile pursuit of climbing Mormond; if I had, I certainly could not have roamed so freely as our forefathers and I might even have come across a group of demonstrators protesting about the NATO base on the hill.

No, I was to be found instead this afternoon at Pittodrie football park, watching Aberdeen, a club which was just one year old at the time of that meeting in 1904. If Gavin Greig had gone to Pittodrie that afternoon he could at least have caught a train to Strichen in time for his meeting. But that main artery has been cut away by Doctor Beeching and we are the poorer for it.

Gavin Greig was indeed a great scholar and it does seem extraordinary that a man of that calibre – and he was not alone in rural Scotland – remained as headmaster of a country school like Whitehill. No wonder Scottish education gained such a high reputation.

I was lucky enough to have a first-hand account of life in Gavin Greig's household from my grandmother, eldest of his nine children, who lived on to her nineties and died not so long ago. It was a house of discipline but it was also a house of good conversation, good music and good fun, all that despite the hardship and tragedy of tuberculosis and so on. Four of his children died in early life.

At that meeting in this hotel one of his daughters, Mary Jane, sang 'Mormond Braes' and he himself had composed an ode for the occasion, called 'On Mormond Hill', which would flow effortlessly from his quill and which ended like this:

> But now the gloaming hour is come
> The breeze dies down; and in the vale beneath
> All by the crooning stream
> The Lammas fields stand deep and dumb
> The shadows deepen over moss and heath
> And far along the shore the great lights gleam
> Downward we take our way till, dark and still,
> The long ridge looms behind. Farewell to
>   Mormond Hill.

At an earlier meeting of this club the members gathered in my native village of Maud, and before they went off to have a look at Brucklay Castle and the ruins of the old Fedderate Castle, associated with Robert the Bruce, they adjourned to my old school (then brand new), where Gavin Greig was again in evidence with a talk which he called 'Lease of Life in Buchan'.

In it he was giving his observations on how life had changed in the Buchan district during the last twenty years of the nineteenth century. Even then he was saying that the old customs were becoming obsolete and the superstitions dying. Within that period, concerts were on the increase but the unaccompanied singer had almost disappeared. Now there was the piano for accompaniment.

In the kirk, the precentor with his pitchfork had been replaced by the pipe organ and full-blooded choir – and the minister's sermon had been shrinking at the rate of about a minute per year until, in 1899 in the more advanced churches, it was down to about twenty minutes!

Many influences had been at work but perhaps the bicycle had as much to do with it as anything; in fact, he said the innocent looking thing was revolutionizing the conditions of modern life and, among other effects, producing a new type of woman with whom man would have to reckon in the near future.

He was greatly struck by the fact that, within that twenty-year period, the Buchan schoolboy had enhanced his capacity for understanding and appreciating wit and humour. He himself, of course, had encouraged self-awareness and further education through his Mutual Improvement Association classes which were so popular in the North-East of Scotland. He used to tell a story of one such meeting where he would give a talk and prompt discussion. That night he asked Jimmy Paterson from Aulfat to start the discussion.

'What's your opinion, Jimmy?' he asked of one who had not been the most diligent of members that evening.

'Weel,' said Jimmy, making a promising start, 'I think ... (changing tone) ... I think ... (changing tone again) ... Damn it, Maister Greig, I dinna ken fit tae think!'

In a fastly changing world, Gavin Greig noticed that Buchan was retaining its individuality better than most districts of the North-East, and he credited the club with having achieved so much in that direction. With the influences which spread across society today, making for a uniformity of life, it is hard enough to detect differences between one part of Scotland and another, let alone parts of Aberdeenshire. Even today, despite the assault of change on the surface of our lives, it seems to me they make a slower impression on the deeper character of the Buchan folk.

As I say, Gavin Greig was observing change in that period from 1880 to 1900. That great North-East writer, Lewis Grassic Gibbon, born in 1901, believed that the rural Scot-

land of his childhood – and many childhoods before him –
disappeared with the First World War. Yet when I read of
the North-East he describes, it seems to me very much the
world I remember in the 1930s. Whereas Grassic Gibbon
thought it went out with the First World War, I thought it
disappeared with the Second.

The people had certainly drained away from the land.
The tractor and bogie now cleared stooks once gathered by
the horse and cart of the thirties, and soon the combine
harvester was to put the binder into the pages of history. I
suppose children of today would hardly know a binder if
they saw one.

My early Buchan was of hairst parks at leading time,
trailing on as a child, more of a hindrance than a help no
doubt but carrying the basket with the piece for my granny,
plain loaf and baps with butter and home-made raspberry
jam and a kettle of tea. We travelled to the moss, too, in
the lea of a cart and brought home the peats from Cowbog,
through the long straggle of New Pitsligo, or Kyak as we
called it, down the Gairdner's Brae and round by Mac's
Yard to Mains of Whitehill.

It seemed like a golden age of school picnics at the Broch
Beach, warm days at Aikey Fair, beer tents and bargains
and the excitement of a thousand horses on that brae of a
July Wednesday, when we savoured the sweet smell of
peace before the deluge of war that swept away my young
illusions, just as that earlier war had swept away Grassic
Gibbon's.

In a lively social scene of the 1930s, I can still remember
my mother dressing up in her evening gown, screwing
ear-rings into her lobes, dabbing scent around her person,
adjusting her suspenders, turning this way and that before
a mirror, in preparation for the Buchan Bachelors' Ball or
the Mintlaw Ladies' Dance.

Meanwhile my father was struggling to fix a thrawn stud
in a stiff collar, with the damned thing skiting across the
floor to the accompaniment of an oath, for which my father

had a particularly rich and colourful vocabulary. I can still hear their voices in late-night laughter at solo parties, long after I was in bed. I can hear the call of 'Abundance', 'Cop', 'Prop' and Misere' and the explosions of disbelief when some incredible coincidence of cards befell.

But soon my golden age of the thirties was tarnished by the black-out of war, a legislation which dimmed all lights but the moon, the glow of the lunar lamp revealing the silhouette of great convoys passing up our coast in the night. The odd ship would sink and we scrambled to Rattray Head beach to gather up tins of sardines, lumps of coal and sheets of cork. From the aerodrome at Longside gigantic bombers took off into the mystery of the night and lent an added air of excitement to a boy's war. Soldiers passed by and billeted themselves in places like Brucklay Castle and Strichen House and the village halls and hotels around Buchan.

In the midst of that war my father came home from the Broch, having kept his regular contact with farmers there, to say he had done something that day he had not done for years. Whereas he preferred to keep his dram till evening, he had joined some farmers for a drink in the Commercial Bar, along the main street of Fraserburgh, that afternoon; a crowded place it was, with the customary bustle of darts and drinking.

After tea that evening, a glow arose in the sky and word soon spread that Benzie and Miller's shop in Fraserburgh was on fire. As it happened, German bombers were over the Forth Bridge and they too saw the glow. Normally hampered by the black-out, they were not slow to accept an easy target for tonight. Up they came, clean over the rooftops of Maud as we cowered beneath the eaves of Park Crescent and trembled at the bumble-bee note which distinguished German planes from our own. On they went towards that glow which lit up the whole town of Fraserburgh and dropped a land-mine – right on that Commercial Bar where my father had broken his rule and imbibed that day. Some of the thirty-one dead had been there since a darts match in the afternoon. Ironically, it was Guy Fawkes Night.

When that conflict was finally over, I found that the childhood innocence had peeled away – no more the safe caress of a steadfast world – but it was hard to apportion blame between war and puberty. The old feein markets had gone and the horses of Aikey Fair too. I believed that the old Scots ways, the songs and the speech and the customs, had gone with the wind of war; but I may have been wrong.

I hear younger people today talking nostalgically about their childhood in the fifties and sixties, mentioning features of life which I thought had gone with the Second World War and which Lewis Grassic Gibbon thought had gone with the First. For certain, the young of today are more interested in folk song than we were in my own youth, and the renaissance in our culture is undeniable.

So the links remain and I am reminded of a letter I received in the aftermath of writing *A Grain of Truth*. It came from an oil-rig in the North Sea and it was written, in beautiful hand, by a man who had unearthed from a drawer at his home in the Braidsea of Fraserburgh the reminiscences of his grandmother. He told me of their content and I gave some encouragement towards their publication. (They were accepted by my own publisher at the time, Paul Harris.) How delighted I was when they eventually came alive in the form of a book, *The Christian Watt Papers*, the diaries and papers of a fisher lassie, describing with skill and sensitivity the life of this area when she would carry her creel up through Buchan and on to Balmoral, where she would meet Queen Victoria and Prince Albert.

It is a story of such hardship and tragedy, ending with forty-seven years in Cornhill Mental Hospital in Aberdeen, as to be almost too much to take. Yet what an inspiring tale of courage and determination, of kindliness and good humour. It is the type of story which helped to forge the Buchan character.

Those of you who have read *The Christian Watt Papers* may have been haunted, as I certainly was, by her description of working in the hairst parks of Strichen House in the days when it was owned by Lord Lovat. There they were, a hundred workers in the field, binding sheaves in the still of a summer's evening, when they suddenly broke into the singing of 'The Lord is my Shepherd'. Can't you just imagine it? A spontaneous choir of hairsting folk, raising a heavenly voice which would filter down over the rooftops of Strichen and up towards the hoosie at the top of Mormond.

It could have been a sound to meet Gavin Greig and his Buchan Field Club members as they descended that August evening for their meeting here in the Freemasons' Hotel. So much changes but so much more remains the same; for we are no more than the children of the children of those people who were here in this hotel those eighty years ago.

Whatever the changes, I believe we are basically the same Buchan folk whose individuality is to be found buried deep in the mysteries of that life in the hairst parks of Strichen House and far beyond. Buried, too, in the ethereal beauty of those voices which rose and wept over Strichen so many years ago.

CHAPTER EIGHT

The Garden of Buchan

In an eventful newspaper career I have wandered far and wide across the world, but the farther I roamed from my native Scotland and the deeper the dimensions that were added to my life, the more I was thinking of Buchan, of the mart at Maud and Aikey Fair and New Deer Show; of the folk who would be swinging up the spring drills or tyauvin' among neeps or silage or redding up a sotter of dubs in the farm close. I could smell the hot dung of cattle in the byre, hear the rustle of the cornyard and sense the melancholy peace of the farmstead on a warm summer's day when a strutting cockerel kept toun and all life seemed to lie somewhere else.

This Buchan which had found its way into the marrow of my bones was an elusive substance to crystallize. On the face of it, Buchan was Mormond Hill and Windyheads, Peterhead and Rattray Head, beef and barley, brose and bannocks; Buchan was Robert Boothby and Aikey Fair, cattle floats and feein' markets, wild sprees at the Baron's Hotel, rowdy dances at Mintlaw Station. Drop down the cliffs at Pennan (where they made the film *Local Hero*) or comb the beach at Aberdour and Buchan was the poetry of J. C. Milne, a whisper in the wind that mixed the tang of the land with the gentle odours of the sea; it was psalms at Crimond and acres of golden sand at Cruden Bay, where Bram Stoker came to create swatches of his famous *Dracula*.

Closer to my own particular focal point, Maud was a lady all douce and respectable on the one hand yet lying in a shameless troilism between her Old Deer and her New Deer. New Deer was the village two miles to the west, higher in its elevation but lower in its tone, a Maud man might tell you, with just a hint of superiority. The main street of New Deer was long and sloped, downwards to the Howe of Hell, you might think, and upwards on a path to the foothills of Heaven, passing through the granite gates of Culsh, where my forebears are to be found in their celestial peace.

Though New Deer in my early days had a fair spattering of folk who were not beyond breaking the peace after a night with John Barleycorn, a native would nevertheless be capable of saying to a Maud man: 'Of course you need three cells in your police station at Maud.'

'Ay, fairly that,' would come the reply. 'But that's only for haudin' folk from New Deer and Pitsligo and tink places like that.'

If New Deer was little more than one long street, New Pitsligo, or Kyak as we preferred to call it, was an even longer worm of a place, home for masons, souters and hawkers, peats from the Moss o' Cowbog, biscuits from Smith's bakery and paraffin and petrol from the kenspeckle figure of Dorothy Park, a lady of ample girth who bothered nobody yet was found one day most brutally and callously done to death. (They never did find the murderer.)

Round yet and you came to Byth, a quaint little rickle of a place with a sense of inferiority, perhaps arising from the fact that a succession of nobility from the seventeenth century onwards, with high-sounding names like Sir John Baird, Member of Parliament, Lord of Session and a Lord of Justiciary, kept disposing of it to each other as if nobody really wanted it. Even up to the twentieth century Byth tended to be represented in the public mind for backwardness, broken down thackit houses, illegitimate bairns and God-forsakenness, a fair sotter of a reputation but a fine bit place for all that.

Not far away, at Slacks of Cairnbanno, my maternal grandfather, Arthur Barron, grew up as a fine, upstanding young man, tall and lean in the mould of Gavin Greig and with so much of a similar interest in local culture that he not only became a willing assistant in Greig's folk-song collecting but an equally willing suitor for the hand of his eldest daughter, Edith.

Together they moved into the tenantry of Mains of Whitehill, just a mile from the Schoolhouse home of Greig, and started their own family of five, of whom my mother was the eldest.

Within the Barron family, my grandfather had a beautiful sister, Betty, married to Willie Park, who took on the lease of Newlandshill of Maud towards the end of last century, and there they raised a large family in the impoverished circumstances of small farming at that time. There was barely enough to meet the essentials of living and certainly not to provide for anything in the way of education. Yet those children of Betty Barron and Willie Park were a highly gifted collection, whose mettle can be gauged from the fact that the eldest son, George, lent the money to put sister Anna through as a teacher; Anna then gave the financial help which put Jessie through as a nurse (she later owned a beautiful nursing home in Edinburgh); the two of them helped Bessie to become a teacher and brother Wilson to become a doctor. And so it went on until the whole family had been given the opportunity to make the most of their talents.

It is not a responsibility that one would advocate for youngsters today, but for those who found the strength and determination to meet the deprivations of poverty in that particular way, there was almost bound to be a reward of character and satisfaction and some measure of success in their subsequent lives.

Perhaps the most interesting story of the Park family was that of Anna. First married to Tom Smith, schoolmaster at Kilspindie in Perthshire, she was left an early widow. Then she married the general practitioner at the ancient village of Old Deer, Dr Ritchie. The marriage took place on the Saturday and on the Monday morning my mother was hanging out her washing when a neighbour, knowing that my mother was a cousin of Anna, came out to say: 'That's very sad about Dr Ritchie. I see his death in the papers this morning.'

'No, no,' said my mother. 'It's his wedding announcement in the papers. They were married on Saturday.'

'Ay,' said Mrs Craig. 'His wedding announcement is there – but his death announcement is there too!'

Dr Ritchie had indeed died within a day of his marriage and

poor Anna was a widow for the second time. By then she had become not only a teacher but a preacher as well, destined to be a legend in the Episcopal Church of Scotland as its first Deaconess, embracing that brand of faith like many more North-East people who felt John Knox went too far.

She found home with her mother in an eerie, rambling house upon a shelf of land opposite the gates of the historic Abbey of Deer, and there we would drive down from Maud on family visits, which I viewed with a mixture of fear and excitement. High among the trees their secluded house, called Newlands, was surely the perfect setting for a Victorian novel, a place of long shadows and weird wails of wind. Sweeping through the corridors of the house in full-length black dress with high collar, Mrs Park still had the bearing and remnants of beauty from her days as Betty Barron.

Still in black, with the white-collared assimilation of a minister, daughter, Anna did nothing to detract from that ghostly air, at least to the impressionable child. Her soft, caressing rattle of a voice and gentle demeanour somehow combined the authority of Heaven with the covert mystery of darker places.

She was the ideal voice of Victorian story-telling and by now, as Deaconess Anna, she was spreading her influence throughout the Episcopal Church, among other things conducting a uniquely imaginative postal Sunday School for children in remote areas. She corrected the homework of hundreds and corresponded with them individually. She became the leader of education in the North-East of Scotland, her power and influence standing in inverse ratio to the noise she made about it.

In time they built a new school in Peterhead, dedicated to the care of handicapped children, and they could hardly have done better than to name it the Anna Ritchie School, a tribute to a quite remarkable woman, though I had never regarded her as anything other than my mother's cousin, a quaint relative who was for ever the Woman in Black.

Tending upon Deaconess Anna, and completing the whole setting of that Victorian novel, was a feeble and faded maid-servant called Isobel, a character straight from Dickens, with straggly hair, streaks of red in her cheeks and eye sockets that were gaunt and mysterious and gave rise to the thought that here was a gentle soul outwith the touch of everyday life.

As if all that were not enough, my childhood visits to Newlands were marked by a most extraordinary event which used to take place on an annual summer day in that picturesque strath which spread itself beneath Deaconess Anna's house, by the Abbey of Deer and the babble of the River Ugie, as it wended its way from Maud and onwards to Peterhead.

Called from our ramblings around the terraced greens and outhouses of Newlands, we would freeze into an awed silence at the sight of a great procession as the Buchan train braked and screeched for its once-a-year halt at a little wooden platform by the foot of Aikey Brae. There it disgorged a teaming array of chanting, white-robed figures who promptly arranged themselves into a parade of the Roman Catholic priesthood, complete with mitre headgear, poised like gaping jaws to the heavens above, before moving off in a prayerful wail of incantation which aroused the tingle of fear and imprinted itself indelibly on the tenderness of the child mind.

This religious pomp in the heart of Presbyterian Buchan needs some kind of explanation. If we think the ruined Abbey of Deer belongs to antiquity, we must stretch the imagination back still further to an earlier Abbey of Deer, which stood by the site of the present Church of Scotland in the village of Old Deer, less than a mile away.

That early monastery was founded by St Columba and his disciple, St Drostan, who came, we are told by legend, on a mission to the Celtic people of Buchan in the sixth century. It was here that the highly-prized Book of Deir was written, now preciously guarded in Cambridge University and containing a splendid record of life in Buchan around the ninth and tenth centuries, with such fascinating details as the shopping-lists of the day.

The present Abbey of Deer nearby was founded by the Earl of Buchan in 1219, as a subordinate house to Kinloss, and flourished for more than 300 years until just before the Reformation. It was run by fourteen Cistercian monks. Two of them came from the south but one couldn't stand the Buchan weather, cauldrif cratur that he was, and the other couldn't bear the uncouth manners of the people.

It may be hard for us today to understand the place which these monasteries occupied in community life, but they were, to all intents and purposes, the local inns, the safest place for a traveller to seek a bed at a time when the highway robbers of Scotland had nothing to learn from the muggers of the twentieth century. In the best traditions of the inn, the monks had a close liaison with a local brewery and were said to be over-fond of the beverage themselves.

The Abbey was in decline before the Reformation, which broke the dominance of the Roman Catholic Church, and some of it had been pulled down by 1560, with local folk carting away the stones. The Abbey contained a church with a nave of five arches in length, transept and choir; that remained standing until 1848 when the proprietor, Admiral Ferguson of Pitfour, the local laird, demolished it and built a mausoleum. That remained until 1930, when the Roman Catholic Church re-possessed the ancient property, demolished Ferguson's mausoleum and handed over the ruins of the Abbey to the Ministry of Works for its preservation.

It was this re-establishing of the links with the Roman Catholic Church which brought forth that pride of prelates in the 1930s, to fix the gaze of Buchan folk, not least the young, in the posture of mesmerized rabbits. Their annual procession was soon to be interrupted by the Second World War, however, and it was not until 1981 that they came again to the lush valley of the Ugie in the Garden of Buchan.

Mercifully, the trouble between Catholics and Protestants, which ravages the beauty of Ireland and simmers bitterly in the West of Scotland, has no place in the life of the North-East. The 700 Roman Catholics in that stretch between Peterhead and Ellon live with their Protestant neighbours in an atmosphere of goodwill.

On the eve of Pentecost, Father Alistair Doyle of Peterhead invited non-Catholic clergy to join the 200 people who gathered in 1981. As a measure of an important occasion, the Abbots of the three Scottish monasteries were there – Abbot Spencer of Pluscarden, Abbot Holman of Fort Augustus and Abbot McGlynn from Nunraw, men of such strict religious orders that they seldom wander from their cloisters.

For me there was a particularly intriguing character involved in that ceremony of 1981. Dom Basil Robinson, a monk of Pluscarden, near Elgin, might have passed unnoticed if I had not discovered that he was none other than the son of the famous Heath Robinson, the English artist whose draughtsmanship poked fun at the machine age, with his hilariously absurd contraptions for such simple tasks as raising your hat, shuffling and dealing a pack of cards or retrieving a stud which has slipped down the back of the neck.

Dom Basil Robinson had devoted himself more seriously to the cloisters of religion, and his artistry included the carving of a plaque for that ceremony, to be erected at the Abbey of Deer.

In the Deanery of St Mary's, which officially describes the North-East corner of Catholicism, what better place for people to share their Christianity than in the Garden of Buchan, with the terraced trees of Pitfour as a theatrical backcloth and the gurgle of the sparkling Ugie for musical accompaniment?

Here, overlooking the ruins from her lawn above, Deaconess Anna once gripped my arm and told me in that voice which seemed to echo from the heavenly places: 'When I waken every morning, I look out on the ruins of the abbey and feel that I must do my best before the day is ended.'

Here indeed, as I gaze upon it now in the latter years of the twentieth century, lies a haven of peace and harmony still, where history seems to linger and listen, as if for the eternal voice of a bygone age.

CHAPTER NINE

A German Provost

Some of my earliest memories of the 1930s consist of gazing hopefully from the top of the Bobby's Brae in Maud and wondering if today would bring the sight and sound of a man whose name added the ring of magic to my childhood.

If the prayers were answered he would suddenly appear in the distance, coming round the Hill of Clackriach from the direction of Peterhead on his motor-bike and yellow side-car. The very thought of Luigi Zanre (we pronounced his name as Louis) stirred dreams of heaven in my young mind, for his ice-cream was a smooth velvet of vanilla, sheer poetry to the palate, and it cost no more than an old ha'penny for a cone.

Luigi's round, smiling face, topped off by jet black hair, brought us the sunshine of his native Italy, from which he had come to Peterhead in 1915 as a lad of just sixteen. And when the long days of summer had shortened to bleak winter, we would travel to Peterhead to the pictures on a Saturday night, to the Playhouse in Queen Street or round the corner to the new Regal, and there we would lose ourselves in the Hollywood fantasy of Clark Gable and Deanna Durbin, Nelson Eddy and Jeanette Macdonald, Fred Astaire and Ginger Rogers. When we eventually emerged to the cold reality of a North-East night, the scent of cinema still fragrant in our nostrils and the balm of Beverly Hills having massaged the imagination, we would call in at the chip shop in Queen Street for a fish supper to last us the journey home to Maud, and there, behind the counter, I would see again that appealing figure of the warm summer days, now in his other role of fish-and-chip man but for ever to be remembered as King of the Cones, Wizard of the Wafer, Lord of the Slider, Luigi Zanre himself.

But soon those safe and comforting days of childhood, reassured by the cushion of two or three generations above, were shattered by the on-ding of war, a mixed emotion of fear and excitement which took time to unravel its bewilderment.

One of the earliest lessons to be learned, however, was that there would be no more ice-cream, not only because the commodities of luxury were now rationed but because the Government, in its precaution of interning all citizens who sprang from enemy origin, had thrown poor old Luigi in prison. We were at war with Mussolini's Italy as well as Hitler's Germany and Luigi was carted off to the barbed-wire captivity of the Palace Camp on the Isle of Man, where he wallowed with others who had failed to change their nationality, including another restaurateur who would later become famous as Charles Forte.

The injustice of imprisoning a harmless friend like Luigi was all the more resented when that same fishing town of Peterhead continued to sport, as its civic provost at the beginning of the Second World War, none other than a German by the name of Max Schultze. The provost had certainly had the good sense to change his nationality – but more of his story later.

In due time the Government felt safe enough to release Luigi and his seventeen-year-old son Joe, who returned quietly to Peterhead and made what kind of business was possible until the end of food rationing.

When I returned to Buchan to mark my half-century, it was one of the true delights to discover that Luigi Zanre was not only alive and well at the age of eighty-two but still battering up the fish in the Queen Street chip shop at weekends, though he no longer ran the business himself. (At the time of writing this book, he is still going strong at eighty-eight.) Nothing less than a rendezvous would do that time in 1981, so we met up in warm reunion at his home in Queen Street, Peterhead, where at long last I caught up with the details of his background. The face, the smile and the shape of the man were unchanged from the 1930s, only the mellowing of jet-black hair revealing that time had not stood still completely.

Though the name Zanre is more French than Italian, Luigi came from the Bologna district to settle in Peterhead when the

First World War was only a year old. Some members of his family were already here, as part of that Italian exodus which went in search of a better living outwith their own long-legged land of sunshine.

As Luigi explained to me: 'My uncle started the ice-cream and they sent me out to the country districts to sell it. There was more money in the country than the town at that time.' By 1921 he was taking the ice-cream as far as the New Pitsligo Games, twenty miles away, with a horse-drawn vehicle. In 1926 he graduated to an open car, and the motor-bike of my early memory was to follow in 1930.

'I was happy going out to the country,' said Luigi in accents which reminded me that he was always better at making ice-cream than speaking English. 'People used to wait for me coming.'

At my own home village of Maud each summer there would be a special delivery for the dazzling Madam Morrison, a French lady who arrived to enliven our sober scene at the end of the First World War, having met our village baker and leading citizen, Captain John Morrison, during battle-torn days in France. When fashionable guests came to visit her from Paris, the glamorous Madam held parties in the luxuriant Morrison gardens, down the back from the bakehouse, and these were not regarded as complete without Luigi's ice-cream, in return for which he recalled being given a handsome glass of champagne.

Madam Morrison, whom I visited in Aberdeen when she was a very old lady but still a vivacious beauty, brought a whiff of Parisian style which gave them something to talk about in the matter-of-fact community of Maud, where you were less likely to encounter French fragrance than the pungent scent of a skittery coo.

So Luigi brought the Madam's order and he never failed to gift his ice-cream to the hospitals in Maud and Peterhead at Christmas and New Year. Then came that war of 1939 when he and young Joe were spirited off to the Isle of Man and, while my favourite Italian did not much like to talk about his internment, he did remember thinking in his captivity that it would have been a specially good summer for selling ice-cream! While his father returned to the scarcities and restrictions which persisted from then till well after the war, Joe went on to join the British Army and serve his family's adopted country with pride.

Quietly in the background of all this, Mrs Zanre, a woman of fine beauty, brought in the coffee and recalled that she had never seen ice-cream until she came to Peterhead. She had previously been Flora Ferrari, aunt of the well-known Ron Ferrari, who departed from his family's traditional livelihood in Peterhead at the news of North Sea discoveries and became one of the modern millionaires of the oil business.

Luigi Zanre had been back to sunny Italy three times in the course of his lifetime in Scotland but always found himself longing for home, which was now in the cold bare blast of Peterhead. Despite the devotion to his adopted homeland, however, Luigi had still retained his Italian nationality. As for that delicious ice-cream, he maintained there was no trade secret beyond the best of ingredients and a great deal of time spent on its creation. Alas, I know of only one ice-cream man in Scotland today who can stand any kind of comparison with Luigi's talents. Happily, his shop is in my neighbourhood on the south side of Glasgow.

To that extent, this permanent tribute to Luigi Zanre can be taken as a kind of requiem for a departed slider, while being at the same time a celebration of the fact that I was able to find its creator still a cheerful and lively citizen of Peterhead more than sixty years after he first tickled the palate of Buchan children.

But what of the German-born Provost of Peterhead? As a young journalist running the Buchan office of the *Press and Journal* in the early 1950s, I was finally able to make the acquaintance of Max Schultze, who had been a name on my horizon since those early war days when he became a figure of sharp controversy over the civic position he held at a time when Britain was at war with his country of origin.

The Buchan folk were keenly divided on the question of Schultze, some refusing to see him as anything but a symbol of the Germany which was now the enemy of Britain and a threat to the peace of the world, others defending a man who had done much for the trade and civic life of the area and was as well established a citizen of Peterhead as any foreigner can be. (Even folk from other parts of Buchan have faced difficulty in being accepted in the Blue Toun!)

In the anti-German feeling of the time, I can recall that my childhood instincts favoured the former view, so it was all the more intriguing to meet the man in person when I arrived as a journalist to live and work in Peterhead. While he had been the Provost in 1939, he was still the town's treasurer more than a decade later, and here, at town council meetings, I found this foxy little figure in John Lennon spectacles, white hair and with a distinctive German guttural in his voice, now well into his seventies but still motivated by a razor-sharp mind which could cut to ribbons the more pedestrian councillors whose stature was purely of the local variety. Schultze, by now calling himself Saunders, was a figure who could have taken his place in the broader arenas of European politics.

I soon learned that he was a capitalist with strong left-wing views, indeed the first Labour Provost to be elected in Scotland, or so I was told.

I engaged him in as much conversation as possible and learned even more about him from that great Victorian presence, Allan Taylor, editor of the *Buchan Observer*, an adversary who once 'chased the little bugger up Queen Street with my stick' but was the first to acknowledge the depth of his culture and the brilliance of his intellect, embodied in which was an impish mischief.

Piece by piece I learned the story of Max Schultze, who was born in Stettin, which was then in Germany but is now in Poland. His father so disliked Prussian militarism that he up-rooted himself and two small children, Max and Charlotte (he was by then a widower), and moved to Britain in 1885, settling in the North-East of Scotland, which had strong trading links with the Baltic. From being a herring importer in Germany, he became an exporter in Peterhead, but they were a family of great substance, well beyond what you might have expected from alien people arriving unknown on the Buchan coast.

Young Max's grand-aunt was the German poetess, Malvinia von Meysenbug, friend of Richard Wagner and the only woman, apart from Frau Wagner, who attended the dress rehearsal of *Tannhäuser*, her account of which was later published in a documentary study of the composer. Malvinia was finally buried beside two more of her friends, the immortal Keats and Shelley.

Max and his sister grew up in Peterhead, Charlotte proceeding to Aberdeen University where she was among the first women to become medical students, gaining a gold medal for excellence in anatomy and physiology. There she met another medical student who was not faring so well in his medical studies, presumably because he was devoting his energies to other matters.

Frank Pearce Sturm, who had family origins in Dufftown, Banffshire, as well as in Sweden, did reach eminence as a physician in due course but later repudiated his success in favour of a life as a poet and mystic, a talented and controversial writer who became the friend and confidant of W. B. Yeats, the Irish poet and dramatist with whom he shared a fascination for the occult.

Sturm, who stirred up fierce controversy in his writings for that memorable North-East publication, the *Bon Accord*, was certainly one of life's extraordinary characters, a writer of such gift that Yeats was moved to write of 'his lovely lines', adding this well-balanced assessment: 'A very delicate sense of rhythm, strange and vivid metaphor. The defect is that the parts are generally so much better than the whole.' He died of a cerebral haemorrhage and coronary attack in 1942, two years after Charlotte had died, aged fifty-six, of cancer.

Meanwhile Max Schultze developed a career in the family shipbroking and herring exporting business, a capitalist interest which would not have seemed to Buchan folk to match up with his passion for socialism; that particular leaning took him to the chairmanship of the East Aberdeenshire Constituency Labour Party and to a position of influence in the wider movement.

At those meetings of Peterhead Town Council where Allan Taylor, a brilliant cartoonist as well as writer, would sit drawing caricatures of local pomposity around the table, Schultze was to be heard cutting through hypocrisy with a rapier for a tongue. Even at his own farewell he rather mischievously rejected the laudatory tributes by refusing to separate public service from private vanity – but that was Max Schultze, lively politician with a wit as sharp as a Prussian helmet and a heart that was so much warmer than he was generally prepared to display.

His son Max volunteered for the Forces soon after the outbreak of the Second World War but felt it would be embarrassing to serve in the British Army with a German name like Schultze; so he changed it to Saunders and his father and the rest of the family followed suit.

Son Max died in 1980, the same year as his mother, but his brother Rudi retains a warm affection for Peterhead from the distance of Bedford, where he is a distinguished gynaecologist.

They lent much colour and variety to our North-East life, these foreign people who came among us around the end of the last century and the earlier part of this. With admirable enterprise, they merged into an alien society and made their mark, whether it was a spirited contribution to the civic life of the area or the sheer gastronomic joy of a slider, for which a little boy in Maud would wait patiently for hours, longing for the sight of that yellow motor-bike.

CHAPTER TEN

From Aberdour to ITN

The humour of Buchan has long been rich and dry, an essential safety valve born of dreich days when not all the drudgery in Christendom could dim the shrewd observation of human behaviour or blunt the fine edge of wit. The unconscious variety was often the best.

I never forgot the minister who was trying to persuade Sandy the Joiner to become an elder of the Kirk. Since Buchan folk are notoriously inclined to accept a modest station in life, Sandy was full of protest. 'Na na, meenister, I'm just a humble joiner.'

'But that's the very point,' said the cleric. 'Just think of it, Jesus himself was a carpenter, exactly like you.'

A new light dawned on his rugged face as Sandy forgot himself and exclaimed, 'Christ, so he wis!'

While I had grown up with the humour and took it for granted, those years as the Buchan reporter of the *Press and Journal* were a rewarding reminder of my heritage. I recall the story of the Peterhead solicitor who went to pay his respects on the death of one of his clients, old John Smith, who had expired after some weeks in Aberdeen Royal Infirmary, on the heights of Foresterhill.

In the customary way of Buchan folk, he was shown through to the parlour to view the corpse and stood in that embarrassed silence which descends on such occasions. Leaving the room with Mrs Smith, he sought to ease the embarrassment with a few faltering words. 'John's lookin' affa like himsel, Mrs Smith, real bonny and peaceful like.'

'Ay,' said Mrs Smith. 'I just said – that last fortnicht in Foresterhill did him a world o' good!'

Further inland, they laughed about Geordie, the Buchan

farmer, whose steading went on fire one night. Neighbours rushed to free the cattle and drive them out of byre and bigging, forming a human chain with pails of water until the arrival of the fire brigades.

At the height of his major drama Geordie paused to wipe the sweat from his brow, suddenly observing a member of the Fraserburgh Fire Brigade with a skin too dark for Buchan. Raising the man's helmet for a closer inspection, he said, 'Faar the hell div ye come fae, min?'

'Oh I am coming from Pakistan,' said the alien fireman in his native lilt.

'Man, ye've deen nae bad,' said Geordie. 'The Peterheid boys are nae here yet!'

Rich humour to accompany a dram on a wild winter's night.

In those days as a Buchan journalist in the early 1950s I unearthed unconscious humour of another variety when, without the usual preliminaries, I was conducted through the gates of the notorious Peterhead Prison, where I spent a week observing and recording the life inside the most forbidding walls in all Scotland.

The Governor of the day, an enlightened man called Major Heron-Watson, gave me a remarkable amount of freedom to talk to prisoners, whose varied reactions to my presence were an interesting study in themselves. Some well-known murderers of the day were frank and friendly, others slunk away with dark looks.

Among the prisoners in Peterhead at that time was a dark, stocky young man serving a sentence for rape, a name which was yet to reach the criminal history books for a series of events which made him the most notorious killer that Scotland has ever known. When they finally caught up with Peter Manuel in his trail of murders from High Burnside, Glasgow, through East Kilbride and Uddingston, slaughtering the Watt family and the Smarts and so many more, there was no second chance of life in Peterhead. They hanged him in Barlinnie Prison, Glasgow, in 1958. (Ironically, while Buchan was playing host to Manuel, a little boy called Dennis Nilsen was growing up in Fraserburgh and Strichen, later to move to London where he admitted the wilful murder of fifteen men, making him the biggest multiple killer in British criminal history.)

In Peterhead Prison the more likeable residents who engaged me in conversation included another legend of Scottish criminal history, the incomparable safe-blower, Johnny Ramensky, of central European origin but brought up in the Gorbals of Glasgow.

Ramensky was such a craftsman in the art of opening the big steel box that detectives were never in any doubt when they came upon the work of the master! So he spent the majority of his years in Peterhead, except during the Second World War when someone in Whitehall had the wit to divert him to more fruitful purpose. Parachuting him behind enemy lines in Italy, they gave him the dangerous mission of bursting open Mussolini's strongroom and stealing vital documents. John accomplished his mission with customary perfection, was honoured for his services to his country – and promptly returned to a life which brought him back time and again to the North-East of Scotland, over-staying his welcome as the guest of Her Majesty.

But if Ramensky (he later changed his name to Ramsay) was a specialist at breaking in, he was equally skilled at breaking out and my childhood days in Maud were punctuated by periodic police activity, as the word went round that Ramensky had again escaped from Peterhead. On one famous occasion, with road-blocks over the River Ythan at Ellon, he speiled hand over hand on the under-side of the bridge as the police checked cars a few feet above. But he would always return, until one felt, on meeting him in Peterhead Prison, that that was his natural habitat.

I was sitting in front of him at a prisoners' concert one evening when a friend of his tapped me on the shoulder and asked if I was the reporter. 'Well, remember that big robbery at the Palace Cinema in Aberdeen?' When I confirmed that I did remember the event quite well, he beamed with pride and added, 'Well, that was me!'

I refrained from offering the hand of congratulation, which he clearly expected, but turned instead to a magnificent rendering of 'Blue Moon' which was coming from the familiar voice of a newcomer to Peterhead, a crooner with a well-known dance band of the day.

The unconscious humour which led me to this topic in the first place came when I was welcomed to the prisoners' discussion group, a lively forum chaired by a former headmaster gone wrong, and sometimes dominated by extremist views which ran from the political to the plain grudge against society. Subjects of discussion included 'Crime in Society' and 'The Problems of Juvenile Delinquency Today', no less!

Perusing the minute book of the group, I was amused to find such items as a welcome for Mr So-and-So; they were sorry that Mr X had now left – but they were delighted to welcome back Mr Y!

The Buchan humour was of a vastly different texture from what those inmates would have known from their homeland in Glasgow and the West of Scotland, where most of them originated. The Glasgow humour always seems to me beautifully encapsulated in the story of the two Glesca Johnnies waiting for a bus in the Gorbals. When it finally arrived, the little conductress called out 'Wan passenger only – the bus is full up.'

The two men pleaded with her to let them both aboard but the wee clippie stood her ground and pressed the bell. As the bus moved away, one of the Glesca men shouted, 'Ach, awa an shove yer bus up yer arse!'

'Naw,' replied the clippie. 'But if you shove yer pal up yours, ye'll baith get oan this bus!'

From the stark walls of Peterhead Prison, which overlooks the spacious Harbour of Refuge constructed last century by a previous generation of convicts, I would drive back round the bay into Peterhead, pondering the weird events of the night and the forces which lead a proportion of the human race to spend the best years of their lives behind bars.

From the office in Broad Street, opposite the illuminated

town clock, I would munch into a bag of Luigi Zanre chips, listen to the late-night background of Radio Luxembourg and phone off my reports for next morning's issue of the *Press and Journal*. The head office in Broad Street, Aberdeen, was staffed by as skilled and colourful an array of journalists as has ever graced a British newspaper, many of whom I have already described in *A Grain of Truth*.

One of the brightest lights in that galaxy was George Fraser, whose delightful prose was being offered to North-East folk in a regular column as far back as the First World War. Imagine my delight, when I went north to tidy up the loose ends of this book in 1987, to find that the same George Fraser was still writing his regular column all of seventy years later!

So I sat down with George at his home in King's Gate, Aberdeen, and caught up with the background of the kind of young man who was liable to become a journalist in those far-off days. Born at Newmachar, where his father was the railway signalman, George was soon flitting north to Buchan, where his father became stationmaster at Longhaven, near Boddam. Peterhead granite was the main export from the local station but the Frasers were on the move once more, first to Drum, on Deeside, and then to Kinaldie, near Kintore. In those days it was left to wise headmasters to persuade parents that a gifted child had to be given the chance of further education. So it was that young George Fraser went from Hatton of Fintry School to Inverurie Academy and then to Aberdeen University, where he graduated MA.

He was marking time for the teacher-training college when he ran into Alexander Keith, a former student friend who would later gain prominence as journalist and author of such books as *A Thousand Years of Aberdeen*.

The persuasive tongue of A.K. diverted George Fraser to thoughts of journalism and that chance meeting in Union Street took him to the office of Sir William Maxwell, editor of the old *Daily Journal*, who told him prophetically: 'Journalists live to be a ripe old age.' George was remembering it well – when he told me the story at the age of ninety-two!

With the First World War at its height, he was one of only four sub-editors turning out the daily paper, handling in particular the foreign news which arrived in the almost unmanageable form of 'flimsy', hand-written and brought down from the Post Office rather like the old-fashioned telegrams.

'The most exciting time,' said George, 'was when we began to get messages about revolution breaking out all over Germany. We knew they were cracking up.'

He was already writing a weekly column when he sub-edited the news of Armistice in 1918. Four years later, when the *Daily Journal* amalgamated with the *Free Press* to become the *Press and Journal*, George became the first chief sub-editor of the new title, the oldest surviving newspaper in Scotland today, with its ancestry dating back to 5 January 1748, and the aftermath of Culloden.

Before George Fraser took up his senior position in 1922 (at the astronomical wage of £9 a week), he had his eye on a girl in the cashier's office.

Young Peggy was already being wooed by a young reporter who wrote her loving verses during his late shifts, but the chief cashier advised her, 'Dinna waste yer time wi' him.'

George Fraser won the hand of pretty Peggy but conceded that the poetry of his rival suitor was powerful stuff, not all that surprising when you find the young reporter was James Leslie Mitchell, destined to become the North-East's greatest ever writer, Lewis Grassic Gibbon.

When I visited them at King's Gate, George was still rising at 6.30 a.m. and cultivating his garden with the same exquisite care that shaped his weekly column in the *Press and Journal*. Peggy, a charming lady of eighty-eight, could still produce with pride the hand-written verses of Grassic Gibbon.

On that same week, George Fraser had been regaling his readers about the origins of that first column in 1918 and how he had been cajoled by Sir William Maxwell. He concluded his article with these beautifully-honed words, themselves a tribute to the sharpness of a man in his nineties:

Happily for me it established to the satisfaction of my mentor the fact that I was capable of putting words reasonably together and of conveying something of what I knew and what I got to know on the long trail ahead.

In time came diversification and a broadening of the harvest field. Some grains of truth, one hopes, have emerged from the preponderance of chaff, winnowed by those favourable winds of chance that have kept me going all these years.

Among the others who had worked away at that same sub-editor's desk in Broad Street, burning the midnight oil as he wrote headlines for my humble offerings from Peterhead, was a man much younger than George Fraser, a fellow-Aberdonian who was destined to be better known in the years ahead.

His name was Sandy Gall, a typical Buchan name, but it was much later before he and I sorted out our common heritage, which extended as far as some common ground in the kirkyard of New Aberdour, where many of our ancestors came finally to rest.

Our rendezvous was far from the sweeping plains of Buchan or the granite sparkle of Aberdeen. It was, in fact, high up in ITN House, a rather unimpressive building tucked away behind Oxford Circus in the heart of London, from which Sandy would come beaming into our living-rooms with *News at Ten* most nights, following those introductory booms from Big Ben.

From the craggy, likeable face, you could almost tell he was a man from New Aberdour, that little village round the corner of the Moray Firth from Fraserburgh, where the beach remains free of commercial influence and the sea gives off that rich tang of dilse I have never experienced on any other coast.

News at Ten was still four hours away as Sandy and I sat in his office raking over our careers and keeping one eye on the teatime news bulletin so he could begin to gather the flavour of what was going on in the world that particular day.

For generations back the Galls were mainly farming folk in the district of New Aberdour, but Sandy's father, the youngest of a large family, went off to be a tea planter in Malaya, where Sandy was born. His father retired to Banchory, sending his son to the prestigious Glenalmond School. In 1945, at the age of eighteen, he became a National Serviceman in the RAF, having just missed the war. Back home in 1948, he embarked on an honours degree course in French and German at Aberdeen University, which preceded his time in the Broad Street head-quarters of the *Press and Journal*. From Aberdeen he went off to be a trainee foreign correspondent with Reuters news agency and extended that experience when he joined ITN, all of which brought a wealth of memories, from the pleasurable to the downright dangerous.

It was trying enough to be covering the Congo War, but imagine his feelings when he was thrown into jail by the soldiers of the notorious Idi Amin and later forced across the jail compound with a sub-machine gun stuck in his back. Mercifully Sandy survived to tell the tale on ITN and to write a book called *Gold Scoop*, which was based on his Ugandan experience.

The horrors of Vietnam and the Middle East War of 1967 were just two more of his adventures before Sandy settled behind the newscaster's desk at Oxford Circus. His routine, I discovered, was to arrive at the ITN studios at three o'clock for a conference fifteen minutes later. His job was then to study film reports arriving in the office and to prepare his mind for writing one or two of the night's stories himself. There was a break between six and seven for a snack or a drink and thereafter the *News at Ten* operation slipped into top gear.

Everyone was busy writing and checking scripts for the vari-ous news items and at half-past-nine, with the adrenalin flow-ing, they settled to a rehearsal. The final pattern of the bulletin was still being thrashed out till the last minute, always making room for announcements like, 'We have just heard that a bomb has exploded in the West End of London. We hope to bring you fuller details in part two.' The uncertainty added up to a real testing of the nerves in one of the few pieces of live television we ever see nowadays.

Before the tension of that evening began to mount, Sandy and I had fair taken Buchan through hand. By then he was Rector of Aberdeen University, an honour which impressed him immensely, as did the maturity of the students and the way the university was run.

'When I went back to Aberdeen I didn't see much change,' he told me. 'But again, I was impressed by Old Aberdeen and the way the university had done so much to preserve the old buildings. Old Aberdeen is really very beautiful and in much better condition than when I was there.'

Every month he took time off to fly to Aberdeen to chair the University Court before handing over to the Principal, Sir Fraser Noble, whose elder brother Donald was my editor on the *Turriff Advertiser* in 1948. By the end of that evening in the ITN studios, the dramas had been performed, the nerves tested and the sweat had run before the closing chords heralded the fade-out and the two announcers exchanged those waggish comments of relief. A chauffeur-driven car was waiting to drive Sandy Gall on the thirty-mile journey to his wife and four children in Penshurst, Kent, a far cry from the gunfire of the Congo and Vietnam and the Middle East, and maybe just as far from the bare braes of Buchan and that rich tang which stirs the nostrils as you comb along the beach at Aberdour.

CHAPTER ELEVEN

—◆◆◆—

Auld Meg Pom

On my sentimental visits back to Maud, I would be regaled with stories from older folk which would stir vivid pictures of life in a bygone age. Old Jimmy Spence had tales of his boyhood days in Maud in the early part of the century and remembered being home during the First World War and taking a dander across the railway line, down through the Low Village and up Bank's Hill. It was a fine clear day and everything was so quiet and peaceful. Yet away down there, far beyond the Hill o' Jock and beneath that same blue ceiling, there were men killing each other by the thousand.

In that same youth, Jimmy Spence, who later settled in Kintore, was walking home with some friends from a dance at New Deer when suddenly there was a loud yell. Somebody had trampled on Meg Pom, asleep by the roadside but soon roused to fill the air with words of blue.

His story sent shivers down my spine, for Meg Pom was still a sight to frighten little children in my own early memories of the 1930s. She and her nomadic brother, Jock Pom o' Leeds (the village of New Leeds in Buchan), went roaming far and wide, Jock with his little cairtie and Meg wrapped in rags and puffing at her clay pipe.

There were few people of the time who did not have a story of coming upon a bundle by the roadside, distinguishable as Meg by the wisp of smoke and the mumblings of one who has had too much to drink. To hear these stories from people like Jimmy Spence and Myra Thow, who grew up at Mid Culsh of New Deer, was not surprising in the context of Buchan life, but the name of Meg Pom (her real name was Park) was liable to crop up in the most unexpected places.

When I left the *Daily Express* in 1980, after twenty years as a sub-editor and feature writer, I spent some time in California, absorbing the life of Hollywood and strolling on the beaches of Santa Monica. A dinner party in Beverly Hills would almost certainly arouse a picture of soft lights and sophisticated conversation, but, lo and behold, I found that my discussion with the lady across the table was about none other than the notorious Meg Pom!

I had met up with long-lost relatives from the North-East, Dr Billy Coutts and his wife Nora, who hailed from Inverurie and Premnay respectively and were visiting their daughter Jennifer, a lady then making a name for herself as the British Airways boss for the whole West Coast of America. The Coutts family were well known for their music on Donside, and once we had given the piano a good dirl, the conversation turned to the vagrant characters who roamed the country roads before the Second World War.

It turned out that Nora Coutts, living nearer the Don, was just as well acquainted with Meg Pom as the Buchan folk who were closer to her origins by the shadow of Mormond Hill. Nora had been so moved by her memories of old Meg that she once wrote a poem, which she recited across that Beverly Hills dinner table and which I am delighted to reproduce here:

> D'ye mind o' AULD MEG POM
> A wifie we wad see
> Lyin' roon the roadsides
> At the back o' Benachie
>
> Like an orra birn o' rags
> That had jist been tummelt doon
> An lookin' oot a facie
> That was ever barkit broon
>
> She'd petticoats an' shawls
> Frae her chin doon tae her feet
> I never saw her lauchin
> But I aften saw her greet

She had anither bunnle
I suppose that was her lot
Row'd in an auld print apron
Tied wi' a muckle knot

Her hair was kind o' tooslie
An' never had a wash
She could hae been rale bonny
But ach, she didna fash

Her auld clay pipe she sookit
'Twas ever in her moo
She lay sae still I winnert
Gin she were deid or foo

In a ditch doon by the railway
Sae quaitly there she'd lie
An' never move a muscle
Fan trains gaed roarin by

But we were richt coorse nickums
We'd creep up tae MEG's lug
An' roar a' we were able
'AULD TINKIE TARRY BUG'

In a trice the auld rags shivert
Her airms cam flailin' oot
She ca'ed us a' the vratches
Ye'd ever heard aboot

Her een noo shone like glaissers
As she tried tae heist hersel
By grabbin' at a breem bus
But back again she fell

We kent she couldna catch us
But feart kine a' the same
We turned an' ran like rabbits
On the lang lang trek for hame

We didna tell oor Mither
We'd roared TINKIE TARRY BUGS

If she had only kent o't
She'd gien us richt het lugs

We winnert faur MEG cam fae
Faurever did she gang
Fan North winds started howlin'
An' nichts grew cauld an' lang

But then cam roon ae Springtime
MEG wasna there ava
Maybe her ain Creator
Had cairtit her awa

Whaur'er she be, I'll wadger
Gin ye speirt fat she wad like
She'd say 'Green grass tae lie on
An' a sook o' my auld clay pipe.'

Versifying about Meg Pom would not have made much sense to the American ear, passing only for the quaint expression of some rustic culture. Yet I knew in my heart of hearts that we were talking about real life and real people.

I knew that, much as I warm to the Americans, the folk of rural Buchan had more true wit and wisdom, downright common sense and sheer smeddum than those pampered floozies of California, so bereft of real problems that they seemed hell-bent on lolling on a psychiatrist's couch and acquiring some.

When I heard them posing such questions as: 'Who am I? Do I know my real identity? I was tempted to tell them, if they had been capable of understanding Buchan logic, that the Scottish farm workers I had known down the years, pulling turnips in the frosty dead of winter with an ache in the back and a drip at the nose, had no such crisis of identity. They knew damned well that they were Wullie or Dod or Davie, working so long and eident-like that there was little time left to dream up imaginary problems on a psychiatrist's couch. They knew there was a wife and bairns to feed and rig for winter and if they had enough left over for a dram on a Saturday night they thanked the Lord that, for another week at least, they had managed to make their frayed ends meet.

Fate may seem to deal out a hand that is uneven and unjust, yet I doubt if the Buchan folk have any real cause to envy the schizophrenic life-style of Tinsel-Town, where constant sun can bake your brain and separate you from reality by the breadth of a dozen Grand Canyons.

I doubt if auld Meg Pom would have chosen the Californian fantasy in preference to her orra birn o' rags and her auld clay pipe.

CHAPTER TWELVE

The Buchan Tongue

The tongue of North-East Scotland, often mistakenly called the Doric, is indeed a language and a law unto itself, broad in its vowels, subtle in its grammar, rich and rollicking in the depth and rhythm of its expression and quite unmistakable in its accent.

It follows the general pattern of what is known as Lowland Scots, as distinct from, and having very little in common with, Gaelic, but it takes the basis of that Scots language and not only broadens everything at least one stage further but has confounded the critics by the fact that it is still in regular use as an every-day speech long after its demise was expected to have been completed.

Well before the days of Robert Burns, the Scots tongue was said to be dying out. More than a century later, Robert Louis Stevenson did not expect it to survive his lifetime yet, in the year of his premature death, 1894, my great-grandfather wrote his most popular vernacular play, *Mains's Wooin'*, which is still performed, understood and enjoyed nearly a hundred years after Stevenson was dead and gone.

Of course no one could pretend that the vocabulary has been totally preserved or that there has not been a dilution of the quality of speech, but the fact remains that it is still there in daily use, nurtured with care and loyalty by the North-East folk themselves and a subject of fascination for the Americans, Russians and Japanese and other nations nearer home.

As far as its culture is concerned, the fact that Aberdeenshire is a wholly lowland region comes as a surprise to many people, even Scots in the southern half of the country, who glibly refer to Aberdonians as Highlanders without realizing there is very little of that culture in the North-East. They themselves, if they happen to live in Glasgow, are much more likely to have Highland origins.

That lowland tongue of North-East Scotland is frequently condensed to a description of 'the Buchan dialect', perhaps because that particular corner of the region typifies its most extreme elements. Of the overseas people who have been intrigued by the Aberdeenshire tongue, the Americans who came by the thousand to participate in the oil bonanza during the seventies had the most practical reason for trying to unravel its mysteries. Once I found myself trying to write a simple explanation for an American oilman who was totally baffled by the niceties.

If he had already learned, for example, that the standard Scots word for 'stone' is 'stane', I then had to complicate life by explaining that Aberdonians further broadened the vowel to make it 'steen'. Similarly, 'bone' to 'bane' became 'been'. That was fairly elementary stuff, just as I assumed the gent had already learned that a 'quine' was a girl and a 'loonie' was a little boy and not a lunatic.

It was more difficult to explain that 'ging' and 'gyang' were subtly different uses of 'go' and that 'gyan' meant 'going'. For example: 'Will ye gyang [go] doon tae the shoppie?' But 'Are ye gyan [going] doon tae the shoppie?'

The English language settles for the single word 'have' but no such simplicity will do in the North-East of Scotland. 'Hae' and 'hiv' are just two of your choices according to the form of sentence. Where an Englishman would say 'You have to have something in your stomach', the Buchan man would say 'Ye hiv tae hae something in yer stamack.' Transposing these two forms of 'have' would sound a nonsense. Yet, change the same sentence into the future tense and it becomes, 'Ye'll hae tae hae something . . .'

When President Eisenhower (commonly known as Ike) came to Balmoral to visit the Queen in the late 1950s, he was greeted by a local newspaper headline which summed up the North-East greeting to perfection: FIT LIKE, IKE?

A North-East response to such an inquiry after one's health

could cause some problems to the foreigner, ranging from the understandable 'Nae bad, min' (Not bad, man) to the more puzzling 'Tyauvin awa' or 'Warslin throu' or 'Knypin on', all three of which indicate that you are working away or struggling along, with the first two giving hint of a harder struggle than the third. Oh, the subtleties of that North-East tongue!

A hard day's work is liable to leave you 'fair ferfochen' (exhausted) and a heavy meal will make you 'fair stappit fou'. If your toe becomes your 'tae', it will be just as painless as your ankles becoming your 'queets'. A knowledge of the German language can be as useful as English when coming to terms with the Buchan dialect. In my childhood, the language of counting was 'een, twa, three, fower, five, sax, seiven, acht'. Aberdonians follow the Germans in telling the time. Whereas 'half-two' in Glasgow or London is just a slovenly way of saying 'half-past-two', the corresponding 'half-twa' means half-past-one in Buchan – half-two being one half of the second hour, exactly as in the German 'halb-zwei'.

On top of all that, Buchan folk possess an absolute genius for diminutives, managing to turn semantics into gymnastics with examples such as 'Little wee bit wifikie', which actually produces five diminutives in a four-word sentence!

And what would the outsider make of this particular conversation in an Aberdeen wool shop, conducted entirely in vowel sounds? The customer is inquiring if her prospective purchase is real wool and all from the same cut:

Customer: Oo?
Assistant: Ay, oo.
Customer: Aa oo?
Assistant: Ay, aa oo.
Customer: Aa ae oo?
Assistant: Oh ay, aa ae oo.

So much for a sketchy background of what the language is all about, a language which lives and breathes as much through its every-day speech as in the richness of its literature. From William Alexander's *Johnny Gibb o' Gushetneuk* through Gavin Greig's novels and plays to the poetry of people like

Charles Murray, the life and language of the North-East have been enshrined for generations to come.

Add to that the unique contribution of Lewis Grassic Gibbon, the North-East's greatest writer, who managed to mould the rhythms of his native corner to the cadences of the English language, and you begin to understand why the special nature of one part of Scotland is becoming more fully understood and appreciated by that wider world outby.

CHAPTER THIRTEEN

There's Aye a Something

If you have an ear for the so-called Doric of North-East Scotland and have ever pursued it through verse, you will inevitably have come across the works of Charles Murray, more commonly known as Hamewith.

Murray was the lad from Alford, in the Donside valley of Aberdeenshire, who rose to become secretary for public works in the Union of South Africa in the early part of this century and spent much of his time nostalgically thinking and writing about the place of his roots.

He wrote in that rich and rollicking style which characterizes the speech of the North-East, with a keen eye for the quirks as well as the qualities of the people. He is remembered for poems like 'The Whistle that the Wee Herd Made' and 'It Wisna His Wyte', and there are purists who will tell you that his technique maintains a higher level than that of Burns.

Certainly his cameos of description are priceless. Just consider the poem 'Dockens Afore his Peers', in which the small farmer is appearing before the labour exemption tribunal in the First World War, seeking dispensation for his son and showing how badly off he is for workers.

He describes the kitchie deem:

She's big and brosy, reid and roch an' swippert as she's
    stoot
Gie her a kilt instead o' cotts, an' thon's the gran' recruit.

For those with doubts about translation, the first line is 'Big and robust, red and rough and nimble as she's stout'. In the next line, 'cotts' are petticoats.

Then old Dockens describes another of his work-force liabilities, the makeshift cattleman:

The baillie syne, a peerhoose geet, nae better than a feel
He slivvers an' has sic a mant, an ae clog fit as weel
He's barely sense tae muck the byre an' cairry in the scull
An' park the kye an' clogue the caur an' scutter wi' the
    bull.

The 'peerhoose geet' is a creature from the poor's house, such a common institution in those days; to 'slivver' is to drool and to 'mant' is to stammer. 'Clogue the caur' means to feed the calves milk from a pail.

Such was the power of Charles Murray. He came back to the North-East from South Africa to retire, and lived there until his death in 1941. Among those who got to know him well was the late Dr Nan Shepherd from Cults, herself a distinguished writer and teacher, who met Murray first when he visited her parents and again when she went to South Africa to see her brother's grave.

Nan Shepherd, who is said to have had a strong affection for the poet (they used to be seen in public holding hands), gave us this description of him in her later life:

Charles Murray was a man one could not miss in a company. He had presence; not self-assertive but dynamic – one felt more alive from being with him. When he spoke he had compulsive listeners. Droll, witty, solemn, seemingly nonchalant but with a delightful relish in what he related, he was a raconteur of genius. He was company for a duke or ditcher and imperturbably himself with both. His lean, hawk face was warm with interest – sheer simple interest in people, what they were, what they did, how they did it.

In an introduction to Murray's *Last Poems*, Nan Shepherd perhaps summed up her feelings when she wrote: 'The seed of Charles Murray's power is that he said yes to life.'

Not everyone was so bowled over by Murray. That other notable North-East writer, John R. Allan, had certain reservations about him, taking the view that his work was more observed than felt.

But few would argue with the appeal of such memorable verse as 'There's Aye a Something', which tells of Sandy, the farmer whose wife is town-bred and genteel and come of folk who thought him 'an unco come doon'. This graphic description of Sandy must surely commend itself even to the most un-Scottish of ears:

> He's roch an' oonshaven till Sunday comes roon
> A drap at his nose and his pints hingin' doon
> His weskit is skirpit wi' dribbles o' kail
> He drinks fae his saucer and rifts ower his ale.

For the uninitiated, his 'pints' in North-East parlance are his bootlaces.

Sandy's offspring have had to take pot luck in drawing genetic elements from their genteel mother and uncouth father, a gamble which Murray sums up in this little gem:

> They're like her in looks as a podfu' o' piz
> But dam't, there's aye something – their mainners are his.

Charles Murray spent those last years in the North-East in the company of a few friends who formed the Sit Siccar Society, with a motto which he penned as a delicious condensation of native caution:

> Be wise an' sit siccar –
> Ye're safe on your doup!

—◦◦—

CHAPTER FOURTEEN

A Great Scot

No mention of Scottish language can pass decently without reference to a man who is still hale and hearty at the writing of this book but who will no doubt have passed on to his Elysian pastures before he is properly recognized as one of the great Scots of the twentieth century. Such is our neglect of those around us.

It was all the more essential that I beat a path to the doorway in Dennyduff Road, Fraserburgh, where I would meet David Murison, a local lad o' pairts whose smallish stature and modest manner tend to belie the greatness within him.

Yet this son of a Buchan joiner went from local schooling to take on the might of Cambridge, gain a double first in the classics and proceed to spend most of his working life in creating for his beloved land that colossal and definitive fount of its language, the *Scottish National Dictionary*. It was a daunting task which called for a scholastic giant with a heart that beat strongly to the rhythms of the traditional Scottish speech, and it was to the eternal good fortune of this nation that such a rare creature emerged in the form of David Murison.

Having achieved his lifetime's work in the same George Square of Edinburgh where Sir Walter Scott had spent his early years, David Murison was now home for retirement in his native corner of Scotland, and there, in his den at Dennyduff Road, I heard again those warm tones of his Buchan tongue, untouched by a life-long barrage from alien forces. David Murison was the same couthy chiel he had always been, as proud as ever of his mother tongue and exercising it with natural ease.

His family came from Wellhowe of Brucklay, apparently ordinary like folk with a genetic streak that was far from ordinary, having previously produced at least one genius,

Alexander Murison, who became Professor of Roman Law in London and a famous jurist of his day. He died in the 1920s and a plaque to his memory is to be found at the Brucklay house where he was born.

David Murison's father was a joiner who went to Fraserburgh to find work. His mother's family came from my own native village of Maud and the boy went to Fraserburgh Infant and Central Schools before his father moved to Aberdeen, again in search of work. After the Grammar School and Aberdeen University, he moved on to his distinguished career at Cambridge before returning to be a lecturer in Greek at King's College, Aberdeen.

The idea of a *Scottish National Dictionary* had first been mooted as far back as 1907 and was eventually taken up by Dr William Grant of Aberdeen. By the end of the Second World War the dictionary was in need of a new and full-time editor and fresh inspiration – and that was where David Murison became the man of destiny for the preservation of the Scots language.

It was a task which was to absorb all his energies for the next thirty years or more. Countless thousands of words dating from 1700 had to be gathered, sifted, checked and double-checked for shades of meaning and usage in different parts of the country before finding their way into the definitive dictionary of the land.

Now that he had reached the final Z, put his *Scottish National Dictionary* to the printer's bed and retired to his native corner, I was interested to know what he had re-discovered about the life and language of the place where he grew up. This was David Murison's view of his return:

I wanted to come back and end my days here and now that I am re-establishing my roots, I have picked up some threads and see faces that are familiar to me, though I cannot put a name to them. But it is sad to come up a street and remember that so-and-so used to live there but is now long gone. The people have not changed. I see the same types. I can remember Fraserburgh just after the First World War when there was a great burst of affluence and a sense of euphoria. Now that has repeated itself with North Sea oil and I am experiencing the same thing twice over.

But the Brochers have not had their heads turned. They have kept an even keel, are still pretty canny and take a sober and serious view of things. They are friendly and still say 'How d'you do?' in the street, even if they don't know you. There are, of course, the unpleasant things, like vandalism, but that is universal. In my day there was harmless mischief but now there is more coarseness in it.

I find that people are alert – they always were – tumbling to what you are getting at with great celerity. They are critical and can size up a situation or an argument and find a flaw in it. Their own speech has changed not very much, with a lot of Scots still spoken, though not so rich. A lot of the vocabulary has gone and there are more anglicisms and American slang picked up from the wireless and television.

But the timbre of the voice is still fundamentally Buchan and I can hear some of the older fisher folk speaking an older-fashioned Scots. The vocabulary does get less, however. Just look at *Johnny Gibb o' Gushetneuk* and you will find words that you never hear nowadays. It was reckoned that, between the end of last century and 1926, about one-third of the vocabulary had gone from our speech. Another third must have gone since then and the deterioration is increasing with television. The trouble is that, with TV and radio, the sound is coming across to affect pronunciation so it reaches you even if you are living in the Moss o' Byth.

Against that, however, it is true that people getting older tend to revert to the speech of their childhood. Just as old memories come back, they remember the speech of their grandmothers and will begin to use the words again. So there is a compensatory swing. But with the trends as they are, our Scots will vanish completely one day unless people consciously and deliberately try to preserve it.

The schools have not helped the position. The educational system has been geared to the furtherance of English and not very successfully, especially now that grammar has gone by the board. There is a great snobbery attached to the use of English in Scotland. Scots has lost social prestige and until you get people out of this fear of dropping social bricks, there is not much hope for it. It was intended to make the *Scottish National Dictionary* available to schools but there has been very little sign of this being taken up. Teachers are apathetic if not antagonistic and only the occasional enthusiast here or there tries to introduce Scots into the culture.

In George Square, where I worked in Edinburgh, the gentry were speaking Scots in the eighteenth century. Then the judges and advocates began imitating the English; the Select Society was formed to acquire standard English and Scots speech had moved to the middle classes.

The rot had set in. The intonations will last for a long time – the vowel sounds and so on. Of course I am a born pessimist; that way I can get only pleasant surprises. But I must admit that, at times, I see a glimmer of hope. It may yet come back into use, as a fashion.

David Murison believes that the so-called inarticulateness of Buchan folk is due to the fact that their speech has been repressed. In the formation of the *Scottish National Dictionary*, however, his own native corner ranked in the top bracket of source material, maintaining a good literary tradition which is still producing its prose and poetry. Other areas which have held to their local speech include the Borders, Galloway, Angus and the Shetlands.

It was David Murison who convinced me that we are misusing the word 'Doric' when we adopt it as a label for our North-East speech. Being the Greek scholar that he is, he reminded me that Doric was the dialect of the Spartans and had to do with roughness and coarseness. The word found its way into the English language bringing the same connotation, and was used by Milton. How it arrived in the North-East of Scotland is something of a mystery, but we seemed to imagine that it applied to us because of our characteristic dialect. This hint of coarseness perhaps explains why so many well-intentioned people talk about 'lapsing into the dialect'. Is it really a lapse?

David Murison spoke it richly and naturally as we sat in his Fraserburgh home and looked across to the Infant School which first set him on his road to Cambridge. The question in his mind was whether or not his life's work would prove to be of lasting value.

Leaving the presence of such a remarkable man, I wondered if Fraserburgh had any notion of the calibre of human being who had come amongst them. Here was such a fount of knowledge about the Scottish tongue as we would certainly never see again. We shall put him on a pedestal one day and say, when it is too late for him to hear it, that we had a truly great Scot in David Murison.

CHAPTER FIFTEEN

Daughter of Grassic Gibbon

For many years of my youth, it would be fair to say, I trod my native scene with little eye or ear for the things around me. It was plain and familiar and generally to be taken for granted. People went about their daily darg with steady gait in a life which seemed dictated more by the bite of drudgery than the soul of inspiration.

Then it happened that, within a matter of days, the whole familiar scene had gained new meaning: the plodding ploughman suddenly symbolized a deeper life that had eluded me; the land that lay still and secretive was adding to its yield of oats and turnips and potatoes a whole new harvest of heritage that was rich and bountiful and nourishing. At last my ears were opened to the voice of that land in which my own ancestral roots were buried, and for all this I had to thank a man called Mitchell – James Leslie Mitchell, better known to the world as Lewis Grassic Gibbon.

I had just read his trilogy of novels called *A Scots Quair*, a remarkable piece of literature which gets at the heart of Scottish rural life and character and expresses it so the whole English-speaking world can understand. The rare technique is that, in order to reach that wider audience, he used a minimum of Scots words which might turn away the outside reader, yet produced a rhythm of Scottishness which left the impression that he had been writing in Scots all the time. It was a language and a feat which belonged to no one but himself.

Mitchell was born and raised in his early years on the very edge of Buchan, at the modest holding of Hill of Seggat at Auchterless, before the family moved diagonally south-eastward to the Mearns, that red-clay district below Stonehaven from which Robert Burns's father had, in his day, moved southward to find work and to settle in Ayrshire.

While his father and mother worked the croft of Bloomfield, young Leslie was travelling down the road to Arbuthnott School, where he was fortunate in the calibre of his headmaster, Alexander Gray. In *A Grain of Truth* I told the story of how he went on to be a journalist in Aberdeen and Glasgow, to spend obscure years in the Army and the Air Force during the 1920s and finally to settle to a life of authorship in Welwyn Garden City, north of London, where he produced sixteen books in less than seven years.

His feverish pattern took its toll, and what should have been a routine stomach operation turned into tragedy when he did not regain consciousness from the operating table that February day of 1935. Lewis Grassic Gibbon was dead before his thirty-fourth birthday, leaving his wife Rebecca, herself from a neighbouring croft in the Mearns, with two young children, Rhea and Daryll. The funeral service was at Golders Green Crematorium and his ashes were brought back to the kirkyard of Arbuthnott, a great light dimmed for ever but not to be extinguished.

The struggle and hardship of the crofting life had raised rebellion within him, but through his anger came an abiding love of the land and the folk whose honest toil had turned it into the fertile base of a decent society. At the same time he could be critical of nearby places like Aberdeen and Stonehaven, and indeed his essay on the Granite City contains such amusing gems as this:

> Aberdeen is the cleanest city in Britain; it makes you long for good, wholesome dirt, littered roadways and ramshackle buildings leaning in all directions, projecting warm, brown sins and rich smutty reds through an enticing, grimy smile . . .
>
> Where Union Terrace breaks in upon Union Street there is an attempt at a public garden. But the flowers come up and take one glance at the lour of the solicitors' offices which man Union Terrace and scramble back into the earth again, seeking the Antipodes.

above: My two grandmothers, Granny Barron and Granny Webster.

right: My father with Paddy.

below: My father in the sale-ring at Maud Mart.

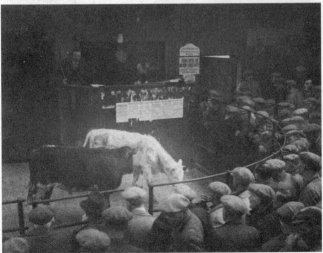

above: Perhaps the first picture ever taken in Buchan – at Inverugie around 1860 – the work of Joseph Collier from New Byth, who became a famous photographer in America.

below: The legendary Lizzie Allan (both legs amputated after a bad childhood inoculation) who ran her sweetie shop from a wheelchair and excited my interest in life.

Rare picture of Strichen's controversial novelist, Lorna Moon.

above: James Duthie, St Combs fisherman turned television playwright.

above: David Toulmin, genuine son of the soil.

below: David Murison, editor of the Scottish National Dictionary.

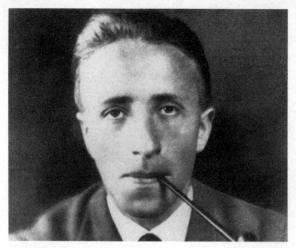

above: Lewis Grassic Gibbon, a unique talent.

below: Rhea Martin, gifted daughter of Grassic Gibbon.

above: Fifty-three years later, I meet up again with Luigi Zanre, still going strong at eighty-eight.

left: Max Schultze, German-born Provost of Peterhead in 1939, when we went to war with the Germans.

above right: As a Daily Express feature writer, in the company of Sophia Loren.

right: Four generations; with my grandmother (Gavin Greig's eldest child), mother and eldest son Geoffrey.

above: With Bertie Forbes, New York millionaire who encouraged me into journalism when he returned for his Whitehill picnic.

left: A generation later, with his famous son, Malcolm Forbes, who resumed the picnic in 1987.

From that base of Welwyn Garden City, Lewis Grassic Gibbon had nevertheless sighed for his beloved North-East, and it was to those leafy lanes of Hertfordshire that I betook myself one day to satisfy a curiosity about the effect of an English upbringing on the children of a great Scottish writer. And there, in the alien tones of a refined English which would have been fair the speak of Kinraddie, Rhea Martin opened up her heart on the subject of her famous father, a man she was really too young to know.

For long, I discovered, she had wrestled with the torment of a memory which lay just beyond her reach and sought to unravel the conflict which made her proud of a distinguished father on the one hand and impatient with some of the consequences on the other. With all the independence and thrawn nature of her ancestral North-East of Scotland, she was determined to be known for herself and not as the daughter of . . .

She need have had no fears on that score. As Rhea Mitchell, brilliant scholar, she studied law at London University, was called to the Bar and became dean of the School of Business and Social Studies at Hatfield Polytechnic, as well as a distinguished legal figure serving on bodies like the Lord Chancellor's Advisory Committee in Legal Aid.

By the time I met her she was already in her fifties, a formidable, good-looking wife and mother to three grown-up sons, one of whom was a Fleet Street journalist.

But to the purpose of my visit: What was it like to grow up as an Englishwoman far removed from the source of her father's life and inspiration in North-East Scotland, with little chance of encountering its language and culture? Could a child of that great novelist perhaps fail to recognize and appreciate Chris Guthrie, his memorable and symbolic character who runs through the trilogy of *A Scots Quair*?

In the calm of that garden city, not far from the house where Grassic Gibbon lived, Rhea turned it all over in her mind and surprised me with some of her revelations:

Do you know, the idea that I was the daughter of a famous author did not materialize as a general proposition in my life until the BBC televised *Sunset Song* in 1970, when I was forty. Other people, including my mother, had told me so but it was not a personal experience for me.

After the television serial, people down here were saying, 'Is it true that you are the daughter of Grassic Gibbon?' When I said it was, their next question was, 'Why didn't you tell us?' But I had no inclination to tell people.

Irked by what she took to be sycophancy, she explained:

I dislike when people enjoy the artificially reflected glory of having been close to someone related to the famous. I find that experience very difficult to respond to because I have such fragile recollection of the things they are being so admiring about. It is a painful vacuum in my life but I have learned to adjust my emotions, to blank it out – not to ignore it – because you have to get on with living your own life.

That fragile recollection arises from the fact that Rhea Mitchell was barely five when her father died on that operating table. So what did she remember?

I have a recollection of sitting scribbling in his study while he was at work in our house at 107 Handside Lane, here in Welwyn Garden, but I have no memory of his voice. I still wonder what his speech was like.

When you have been told anecdotes so many times they become part of your memory, so it is difficult to know what I do actually remember about him. I have a recollection of my mother telling me something very solemnly and I can only imagine she was breaking the news of his death.

I first read *A Scots Quair* when I was about fifteen or sixteen but found it difficult because I felt under an obligation to read it. However, I still take the view that the emotions expressed are very hard to understand at fifteen, and I am not sure it should be O-grade material in the Scottish schools. I think it is too early.

I don't think I knew the character of Chris Guthrie and I found I had absolutely nothing in common with her. Yet some people say she was modelled on my mother and that made it difficult for me to read about her objectively. So there was a long time I didn't read the books at all. But last year I wanted to take a fresh look at them. They were doing a musical version of *Sunset Song* at the Edinburgh Festival and I took a paperback version of *A Scots Quair* up with me and read it again and enjoyed it best of all this time.

I wondered if any of Grassic Gibbon's writing urge had been passed on to his offspring.

People say I have a talent with words but I use it more in speech than in writing. I used to cringe when people asked me if I was going to grow up and write books like my father. It was very inhibiting and I didn't know what the hell they were talking about! I had no interest in writing novels, partly because I had turned my back on it all. I was being asked to emulate someone I didn't know and was always suspicious of that since I am very much my own person.

Struggling as a young widow with two children to bring up, Rebecca Mitchell (she came to be known as Ray) went back to the Civil Service and young Rhea was sent to Christ Hospital, the charity school which kept some places for the children of deceased people who had had some distinction in life. Compton Mackenzie and Ivor Brown had a hand in the matter. She remembered arriving there in September, 1939, at the outbreak of war, and tucking her gym slip into navy knickers for the very first job of filling sandbags.

Brother Daryll was sent to the famous A. S. Neil's free discipline school at Summerhill, but they were re-united with their mother at holiday times, when they headed for Scotland.

My mother had to breathe her native air so we stayed with relatives and I had to go out to play with cousins I could hardly understand – and they couldn't understand me.

There was a slight resentment about the Mitchells who had gone off to live in England, almost as if we had manufactured airs and graces to which we had no claim.

On one of our visits to Scotland we stayed with a family called Crawford in Dundee. We went into a tea-shop one day and Mr Crawford, who had known my father, called over another man and introduced me as Lewis Grassic Gibbon's daughter. What I received from this man was a tirade which made it clear he was not an admirer of my father. It was the first time I had heard anyone speak against him. Mr Crawford then told me he had done that deliberately because he felt I should know that not the whole world was pro-Grassic Gibbon.

Whatever the charity of that, it was of course true that many people, unable or unwilling to appreciate the poetic genius of the man, were ready to take umbrage at his forthright observations. Had not his own mother been tempted to ask what he was writing all that 'muck' for?

What of the Scottishness which must surely have lurked somewhere in the genes of Rhea Mitchell's Pictish parentage?

When my father died, a number of people encouraged my mother to take us back to have a Scottish upbringing but she was not prepared to move. My own view about being Scottish is, I suppose, much the same as that of people who emigrate to Canada. Once you are out of Scotland, the distance doesn't matter. People are glad to say they come from Scottish parentage. It is nothing to hide but it is nothing deeper than just that.

Since the death of her mother in 1978, I suspect that Rhea Mitchell, married to a delightful Englishman, Gill Martin, an engineer who gave up work early through ill health, has found herself with the new responsibility of keeping the ancestral threads intact. She acknowledged that there was a basic instinct to do that.

Just as her father was cremated at Golders Green and his

ashes taken back to Arbuthnott in 1935, she followed the same routine for her mother, placing the ashes under the same headstone which bears those moving words from the closing passage of *Sunset Song*:

> The kindness of friends
> The warmth of toil
> The peace of rest

Ray Mitchell had been bitter about losing her life's partner so young, feeling his death could have been prevented. Her own life was spent in furthering his name, when publishers and public were in shameful neglect of him. (In the 1950s I joined with her in badgering publishers about bringing his work back into print.) Now they were together again, back in the red clay of the Mearns which had given them both roots and an early contact with each other.

That noted Aberdonian poetess, Nan Shepherd, mentioned in a recent chapter, was present in 1978, as she had been for Grassic Gibbon's own funeral in 1935, remarking on how completely similar the two services had been.

They played 'The Lord's my Shepherd' and closed the service with 'The Flowers o' the Forest', just as Grassic Gibbon had closed *Sunset Song* with the piper playing the lament up there by Blawearie Loch.

That same day, Rhea's journalist son Alister, from Fleet Street, found himself gazing at the land and its people and appreciating for the very first time what his grandmother had been speaking about throughout the years.

Rhea herself came back to that Edinburgh Festival with no intention of visiting the Mearns. Then a strange thing happened:

When I was there I suddenly felt a strong requirement, not an obligation, just a 'requirement' within myself to go back. So I drove up from Edinburgh and back again without speaking to a single soul. And I wondered why I had gone because there was no one left to visit. But it is a peaceable place and it satisfied something within me.

Her face glowed warmly, like the rich soil of the Mearns, as she spoke of it. It was the tug of a tradition which had ensnared her father without yield and produced great literature from the distance of Welwyn Garden City. There she stood alone at Arbuthnott, like Chris Guthrie at the standing stones of ancient times, listening to the grey North Sea as it rumbled beneath the cliffs.

The gaze of Grassic Gibbon's daughter spread across the Mearns, with its red clay soil and modest crofts, reaching to the foothills of the Grampians and rising into the western horizon of a summer's evening; rising into the glow of a Sunset Song which echoes like a distant melody in the human heart.

CHAPTER SIXTEEN

Trauchle and Triumph of Toulmin

My joyous ramble over Buchan revisited was bringing me, more than I had intended, into the company of people who were expressing themselves in words of one kind or another.

But the contact was as rewarding as it was inevitable, especially on such an occasion when I crossed outwards from the Buchan boundary to renew acquaintance with an exile who had gone to the city of Aberdeen. Driving down one of the streets which lead to the Pittodrie Stadium of Aberdeen Football Club, I found myself at the fireside of a man who could be described as a unique figure on the Scottish literary scene.

I had come to visit David Toulmin, an old-time farm servant who was thrust into publication when approaching his sixtieth birthday, with a book of stories from his observations of country life. Not that his projection into the limelight of acclaim was resisted by any means; indeed it was something that might have belonged to his private dreams, but, with the curse of self-effacement which besets the Buchan breed, the transfer to reality would have seemed an unlikely proposition.

For here was no phoney farm labourer who might be concealing some university background. Here was a genuine, 100-per-cent son of the soil, a ploughman born into an Aberdeenshire cottar house and sired by a father who could not sign his own name.

It was a bare childhood in the grey, dreich setting which had been the farm servant's lot for generations, moving from school to school in the Buchan area according to his father's latest 'fee'.

But David Toulmin, whose real name is John Reid, had a sensitivity of soul which stirred dreams of a romantic world beyond the fairm-toun, with its dubs and drudgery and siccar code of unrelenting hard work. Even if that other world were not a haven to which he could readily escape, there was at least nothing to stop the humblest human from entertaining his flights of fancy. At the Playhouse Cinema in Peterhead he absorbed the glitter of early Hollywood and proceeded to write his own little stories, passing them cautiously round the chaumer where he and his fellow farm servants bothied.

There was little privacy to continue his writing but, mercifully, the bite of the turnip field in winter and the numbing thistles of the cornyard at harvest time did nothing to blunt the sensitivities of David Toulmin, who worked on the farms of Aberdeenshire from the day he left school at fourteen. He kept a diary and recorded not only the life and work of the fairm-toun but the thoughts and feelings of one who might have come to be regarded as a bit of an oddity had he revealed to his fellow workers the true extent of his delicate pursuit. Such tenderness might have seemed out of place amid the tang of sharny cattle and the earthy talk which characterized rural life.

However, he still managed to adorn the chaumer walls with pictures of Marlene Dietrich and Greta Garbo, a custom quietly noted by Margaret, the kitchie deem at Newton of Kinmundy, near Peterhead, when she went to make the men's beds. Margaret was maybe no Garbo or Dietrich but neither would Garbo or Dietrich have been much of a Margaret when it came to milking kye or baking scones or reddin' oot the chaumer. So Toulmin put his celluloid fantasies to one side and married her and they settled in a cottar house at Newseat of Peterhead, where his daily labours as a dairyman produced those same little bottles of milk which we awaited so eagerly at Maud School when Duncan Davidson's van arrived at 11 o'clock.

With privacy thus restored in a home of his own, settled in marriage in 1934 at the age of twenty-one, he could write again, and in time the *Farmer and Stockbreeder* accepted his modest offerings on animal husbandry and paid him five guineas, which was a good deal more than you were paid for mucking nowt in a byre.

But the prospects of a writing career remained fairly remote for a man at the hard end of the working scale, without any contacts in the distant realms of literature. He read his way through the whole of Shakespeare (except *Love's Labour's Lost*), then chanced upon the wonder of Lewis Grassic Gibbon, whose books inspired in him a fresh burst of activity. But Toulmin was approaching fifty before his stories and recollections, expressed in the native rhythms of Buchan, saw the light of day, even in his own local newspaper in Peterhead, the *Buchan Observer*.

From there they were spotted by a Buchan man at the BBC, Arthur Argo, who arranged for them to be broadcast. Then, in 1972, the imaginative young publisher, Paul Harris, then functioning in Aberdeen through his Impulse Publications, brought out that first collection as a book called *Hard Shining Corn*. It was so well received as to send some critics into comparisons with Grassic Gibbon himself. If that was stretching it too far, it did at least help to spawn a successor, *Straw into Gold*, and then, at the age of sixty-three, Toulmin wrote his first full-scale novel, *Blown Seed*, in which the talented farm servant wrote passages like this:

Now the soft wind carried the seed over the parks, tiny motes in the sunhaze, each one its parachute of lighted down, blown seed in the wind, showering over the crofts and the farms like snow in summer, sprouting in a year or two where folk scythed and hoed to keep their crops clean.

The paperback rights were sold before the hardback edition was even published and, as we sat by his homely fireside that day in Aberdeen, Toulmin regaled me with the story of how he was fêted by the London paperback people at the Station Hotel, Aberdeen:

They took us to dinner but before we sat down the chief salesman went away to check up on the latest figures. He came back to announce that, in less than three weeks, they had sold 16,000 copies. They had to bring me a chair till I recovered!

Toulmin, now roused like a frisky stirk by the revelation of his own potential, began to harbour thoughts of blockbusting success, and he and Margaret, a fine, homely body of plain dignity and charm, wondered quietly if he had made it at last to the best-seller bracket. Since *Blown Seed* unveiled some of the sexual life of the countryside, had Scotland perhaps produced a Harold Robbins in tackety boots?

That early selling promise was not exactly fulfilled but the paperback company came back for his next book, *Harvest Home*. In 1980 he parodied Robert Louis Stevenson and wrote *Travels Without a Donkey*, an account of the journeys which he and Margaret had made around Britain since the day he was able to afford a motor car. During a decade of literary success, David Toulmin left the trauchle of farm life and moved to the refinement of landscape gardening in Aberdeen, settling himself in that street where the football crowds stream past to Pittodrie. And there he continued his writing, with more time and comfort at his disposal, till he retired from all kinds of manual labour. He suffered periods of deep depression for which he sought treatment, and by the age of seventy he was telling me that he had written his last book. With rural matter-of-factness, he said: 'Tae tell ye the truth, I'm scunnert o' writin'. It's gettin' tae be a trauchle. Fin I sit doon at the typewriter it's like sendin' me tae pu' neeps.' Mercifully he survived that state of mind and has since produced other books.

In 1986 his appetite was sufficiently revived to give us more sketches of life and characters from his native corner, under the title *The Clyack Sheaf*. In farming terms, the clyack was the last-bound sheaf but not the end of harvest altogether, and therein lay the hope that we had not seen the last of Toulmin. His writing has retained that ingenuous touch you would expect from a man who has riven with nature all his days, facing the hard facts of a demanding life without any expectation of a favour.

Some might hint at early deprivation and say a man like Toulmin would have gone further with more schooling, but I suspect that his raw talent might well have been impaired. In the Scottish system of his day, rural children were remarkably well educated by the age of fourteen (Grassic Gibbon had no more favourable a start) and Toulmin made it his business to acquire books which took him well beyond that level.

In *The Clyack Sheaf*, he went back to visit some of the places he knew as a young farm servant. As a starting point he returned to Greystone farm, near Peterhead, and was met there by farmer Willie McIntosh, on the very spot where Willie's father had engaged him as a loon to work the orra beast and sort the nowt fifty-six years earlier. He took us on through the country life of his younger days resuscitating characters like the flamboyant Baillie Booth, Buchan farmer and butcher and the man who went north to the Orkney sales of 1923, bringing back a piece of livestock with a difference – Robert Boothby, who would spend the rest of his career as Tory Member of Parliament for East Aberdeenshire.

Though firmly on the other side of the fence, Toulmin was not short on his fascination with local lairds like Doctor Bruce of Inverquhomery, who happened to be one of the most eminent medical men of his day, pioneering the study of psychiatry, neurology and multiple sclerosis. He reminded us (if ever we knew) that Rafael Carlos Gordon, laird of Wardhouse, at the back o' Benachie, was so closely involved in the affairs of Spain that he practically ruled the country in 1931, when King Alfonso was dethroned. He was then forced to flee from Franco.

He touched on the living poet of Peterhead, Peter Buchan, and the dreaded Miss Mackenzie of Foveran House, who lived reclusively in her mansion until 1973, having once studied music in Germany and frequently had tea with Hitler at Berchtesgaden. But he never strayed too far from grubbing the hill park or hyowin the neeps, mixing his English with Buchan phrases which came as naturally as his stride down the greip with turnips for his beloved cattle.

David Toulmin saw his first tractor at work in 1928 and a

decade later it was intruding upon the domain of the work-horse. In time the machine made obsolete his own labours of nearly half a century, and it was then that he withdrew gracefully to that job as a landscape gardener in Aberdeen, 'where I was privileged to finish my working life in pleasant surroundings, which made a gentle art of my former agricultural experience.

'I got out of farming at the right time,' he said as we looked back on his life and times. The years had not softened his distaste for the grey pleiter of farm work; yet, ironically, he could say in all honesty: 'I'm glad I did live in that manual era instead of working with those new-fangled tractors. There was more camaraderie and the world was a happier place.'

So Toulmin found himself in the same predicament as Grassic Gibbon and many others – writing about a life of drudgery and sometimes despair, yet doing so with not a little affection. That land still tore at him like a nagging love, so deep and abiding that you could rail against it with the full force of your vigour, in the certain knowledge that you could not bear to be free of it.

CHAPTER SEVENTEEN

—◦◦◦—

The Scribe of St Combs

The beach by St Combs stretched like gold against the clear blue sky, punctuated by that column of cement blocks which still stood poised in anticipation of Hitler's tanks.

My mission as I drove towards that cluster of fishing villages on the Buchan coast was to find a man who had intrigued me in recent years, a man just born as that German crisis was reaching its height. James Duthie had been a fisherman from the day he left school in Fraserburgh in 1957, steaming first to the herring grounds and later to more distant waters where they fish for pilchards or whatever comes their way. While plying those varied waters this typical Buchan fisherman who claims, without boast, to having been 'rale thick' at school was scribbling in the dead of night and giving shape to a most extraordinary play for television.

When he took his courage in his hands and marched up to the BBC with his script, they blinked with new respect for a man who scarcely looked the part. They did indeed make it into a strangely haunting and beautiful television play called *Donal and Sally*, which dared to tread on the sensitive ground of two mentally retarded youngsters falling in love. That was followed by a shorter but no less perceptive piece of television drama, *The Drystane Dyker*.

What sort of a man, I wondered, was producing those delicately observed dramas while pursuing the harvest of the sea as a means of livelihood? James Duthie was already at the door of his house to greet me as I drove into St Combs, looking every inch the rough-hewn, weather-beaten fisherman and much less the playwright. It was a reassuring start. The lean and angular appearance and lilting fisher tongue were reminiscent of Fraserburgh fishermen I remembered from as far back as those days when we boarded the train at Maud Station with an unbearable anticipation of the school picnic which would take us to that magnificent beach stretching round from the Broch towards the point at Cairnbulg.

James Duthie was born in 1942 of a Fraserburgh father and Cairnbulg mother and brought up in Watermill Road, though his actual birth took place in the aristocratic setting of Haddo House, family seat of Lord Aberdeen, which was turned into a hospital during the war. At the age of fifteen he followed the tradition of the sea as tenth man on a fishing boat, remaining there for twenty-three unbroken years until he said goodbye to his mates of the *Sedulous* and came ashore in 1980.

The years between reveal a classic tale of what can be achieved when your heart has set its objective. For James Duthie was no academic. Grammatic writing, as he said himself, was beyond his capability. To him a dangling participle was something which needed surgical attention. But he did have the urge to be a writer.

Claiming that he shared a birthday with Shakespeare, he was soon testing me out with his solemn-faced wit: 'I think I'm better than Shakespeare. He couldna write for television. Of course, the English will tell you there wisna television in his day but the English will use anything as an excuse.'

Jokes apart, James Duthie knew that, in the absence of grammar, his concentration must be on the dialogue of drama, where very little grammar is expected. So he sat down to write his play, all the time wondering who there might be to advise him. That was where fate took a hand. While unloading catches at Shields, in the north of England, he discovered that a gentleman who often came to collect fish at the market was Tom Hadaway, one of the writers then engaged on that popular television serial *When the Boat Comes In*.

'I introduced myself and said I could write better plays than you see on television,' said James Duthie. It was the kind of stray remark we all make after some dismal drivel on television but Hadaway knew that Duthie really meant it.

'He advised me to write in the dialect and to pick a subject I knew something about, a situation I had seen for myself. Well, there was a woman who used to live beside us in the Broch and she was handicapped and her boy-friend was the same. He would come up to see her, swinging round the lamp-posts as he came, but she would let him in only if he had a bag of sweeties.'

Thus the seeds of *Donal and Sally* were sown, with Duthie developing his personal observations through visits to the Willowbank centre for handicapped people in Peterhead, where the play was eventually filmed, using a mixture of professional actors and handicapped people. The actual script took only two or three days to write; then Tom Hadaway lent his advice and put him in touch with the appropriate producer at the BBC in London. What seemed like a risky undertaking ended up as a memorable piece of television drama.

James Duthie hovered behind the cameras as they filmed, bemused that the brainchild of a working fisherman was actually receiving this kind of attention from actors, producers, camera crews and so many more. He regarded the fee of £950 as proof in his hand that he had made it as a writer, albeit without any knowledge of technicalities like grammar.

An encounter with an old-fashioned drystane dyker on Deeside was the inspiration for his next attempt at television drama, and that survived a period of cold storage to become another success on screen. What finally brought James Duthie ashore was a commission from the BBC to write a major television series which was intended to do for the North-East of Scotland much the same as Tom Hadaway and *When the Boat Comes In* had done for the North-East of England. He gave it the title *The Buchans of Buchan*, the story of a fishing family with a look at the traditional values, set alongside the values of the modern day.

'We have lost a lot on the way,' he laments. 'The fishing community today is not so close-knit as it used to be. The great god money has taken over.'

But there is still a recognizable way of life in places like Inverallochy, Cairnbulg and St Combs, an atmosphere of the true fisher folk, with faces that are etched from the experience of a fickle fate, triumphant one moment, tragic the next, calmly resigned to whatever the gods may decree. James Duthie's grandmother was one of those people, living in the last house in Cairnbulg to acquire electricity and still carrying water when she was in her eighties, not so long ago.

The BBC paid him for his first six episodes of *The Buchans of Buchan* but, paradoxically, the commission which brought him ashore to the life of a full-time writer was later shelved and has not yet seen the light of day. James Duthie conducts his correspondence with the BBC in the Buchan dialect and has been known to storm the sophisticated Television Centre in London with a splendid disregard for the language and sensitivities of the English. As a left-over from his days of reading and writing while the boats were searching the fishing grounds or heading back to port, I discovered when I intruded on his routine on that bare Buchan coast that he had still retained the nocturnal habits of working. Nowadays he was catching words instead of fishes and wandering along that lonely shore by day, dreaming up his dramas.

His wife, Margaret, and children, James and Margaret, know him better as a fisherman but seemed to attend respectfully on his new career. They are all fisher folk from St Combs who have been going to sea in little ships for generations. No matter what height of literary success may be achieved – and he deserves so much – that is where James Duthie and his family will always belong.

CHAPTER EIGHTEEN

Moon over Mormond

Motoring through Buchan on this mission of rediscovery, I was turning over in my mind some of the great worthies I remembered from childhood days, people like Sandy Wilson, the Strichen horse dealer; John Dickie Dempster, rugged farmer and calf dealer who regaled us with the gossip of the district in our house at Park Crescent, Maud; Johnny Robson, the Carrot King who could fair make the melodeon dance and was better known as Johnny Naeman, from his quaint habit of muttering to himself 'Nae man, nae man'.

Most warmly of all, perhaps, I remember Lizzie Allan, who ran the sweetie and tobacco shop in Timmer Street, Maud, from the seat of her old-fashioned wheelchair, having suffered amputation of both legs as a little girl. As I described in *A Grain of Truth*, Lizzie dispensed politics with peppermints, philosophy with fags, a powerful magnet of a woman who held court in the paraffin-dim bleakness of her timber-built shop, mesmerizing with the clarity of her mind, the whiplash of her tongue. To me she was Boadicea in a bathchair, riding through life with a rare majesty when all the forces of humiliation were ranged against her. She excited my interest in life but it was only recently, when acquiring some early photographs from her half-sister, Ada Stott, that I realized what a truly beautiful woman poor Lizzie had been in her day.

The modern propensity for self-examination and the exposure of every quirk in human nature militates against eccentric behaviour, so we resign ourselves to the fact that the great characters belong to another day and age. Yet I was meeting people of my own generation who had developed strengths of character and powers of personality which could not have been foreseen when I knew them as youngsters. Perhaps we need to reach a certain level of age and experience before those added layers begin to come through; indeed it would be astonishing if the processes which have survived the long history of human development came suddenly to a halt in our own generation. So there are still eccentrics in our midst today (or worthies, as they call them in the North-East), and the destination of my drive that day would set me down at the door of one of them.

Bob Bandeen of Strichen had survived two coronary attacks, a cerebral haemorrhage, a major stomach operation and goodness knows what else, but was still in such good fettle as to joke about the fact that there is a lot of killing in a kyaard. The Bandeen home was The Cloisters in Strichen, a house as unusual as the man himself inasmuch as it used to be the Roman Catholic chapel of the aristocratic Fraser family, who later became the Lovats. His living-room rose in steps to the altar and there was even a pedal organ to round off an atmosphere of peace and contentment.

I had first known Bob Bandeen at the end of the Second World War, when he came to make a kilted skirt for my mother; but then Bob was always making something. He had made breeks and waistcoats for the Duke of Windsor in his days as a tailor in Insch. Though he left school at the customary age of fourteen, he had been in his time a teacher, tailor, soldier, preacher, dance-band pianist, toolworker, librarian and anything else you cared to ask of him. Bob was never stuck, and what he didn't know, folk said, he would damned soon make up. During the Depression of the 1930s he worked as a navvy while perfecting his knowledge of Latin, Greek and Hebrew at the same time.

They used to tell some wonderful tales about Bob, some of them apocryphal but most of them perfectly true; like the day he was on his way to play the organ at Insch and fell off his bike on the ice, ending up with a wet backside. Hurrying on to the kirk, he sought to hasten the drying process by leaving his shirt tails flapping outside his trousers to gain benefit from the wind. As the minister waited anxiously for his organist, a breathless Bob arrived at the kirk, proceeded to march straight through from the vestry – and convulsed the congregation with the sight of his sark tails still flapping behind him!

On another occasion, he was accompanying a much-remembered Strichen minister to a social gathering where his reverence commented upon the early physical development of young girls in the modern world.

'Ay, minister,' Bob is alleged to have replied, 'there's mair uplift in yon lassies than in maist o' your sermons!'

Bob acknowledged the stories, and took me back to his early days in Aberdeen, where he attended Westfield School, at the corner of Esslemont Avenue and Whitehall Road. Being 'the feel o' the faimily', as he liked to describe himself, he served his apprenticeship with his father, who had a tailor's shop in Leadside Road and one in Skene Square. But Bob got the dirty jobs to do, so, as soon as his time was served, he moved out to that rural tailor of great renown, Russell of Insch, who served royalty and millionaires as well as local folk.

'The Royal Family would come over tae Russell's on a coorse day when they couldna get oot an' aboot,' Bob recalled. 'Queen Mary used tae come and the Lascelles family and the Duke o' Windsor; but nae Mrs Simpson. They used tae hae a glorious rake roon and they aye bocht something.'

But there were long periods of unemployment in the winter months and Bob navvied and played the piano in a dance band, taking lessons in his spare time from a Highland schoolmaster who sharpened up his knowledge of Latin and Greek.

Greater security came with the offer of a job as dairyman at Nether Cortes of Lonmay, but it was 1939 and the war was on. Bob remembered it well: 'I joined the Home Guard with the laird and big Norman Murray, the heavyweight athlete, and we were stationed on the edge o' Cortes Lake. But we couldna live for midgies so we decided tae gie Hitler a scare and jine up. We gaed tae Saltoun Place in the Broch but didna expect tae be called up. Inside a week, however, the laird was awa tae the Air Force, Norman Murray was in the Navy and I was in the Army.'

I have long been convinced that the magnetism of personality attracts experience so it was no surprise to find that Bob Bandeen was seconded to Intelligence and drafted into that extraordinary emergency when Hitler's deputy, Rudolf Hess, landed in a field at Eaglesham, near Glasgow, in 1941, on the eve of Germany's attack on Russia. Hess had come to plead the cause of a negotiated Anglo-German peace, prompting Churchill's comment: 'The maggot is in the apple.'

Back in Buchan after the war, Bob went to the Training Centre in Aberdeen to gain a teaching qualification, meeting up with J. C. Milne, the lecturer who wrote *The Orra Loon*, and who told him 'We never turn onybody awa fae the troch.'

Bob Bandeen was appointed librarian at the village of Strichen with the princely salary of £156 a year, with £20 a year for an assistant and £20 for a cleaner. His wife became both and, while he regarded it all as a matter of genteel poverty, it was at least a job in which the Bandeens could be completely happy.

That howe of Strichen which was home to Bob and his family had produced many fascinating tales in its time and I was particularly interested to know what part he had played in the modern reprinting of the novel *Dark Star*, which was written by a famous daughter of Strichen, Lorna Moon.

Lorna Moon was the pen-name of Nora Low, whose father was Charlie Low, a well-known Strichen personality and one of the early Socialists who used to organize meetings of the Fabian Society on the market-stance. The Lows had the Temperance Hotel in Strichen and it was a commercial traveller who happened to pass that way, a William Hebditch from Selby in Yorkshire, who fell in love with one of the daughters of the inn, Nora Low. The pair eloped to be married by special licence in Aberdeen on Christmas Eve of 1907 before emigrating to rural Canada. Nora had one child by Hebditch but the restless spirit of the budding writer was soon on the move; she left home for the city life, met up with a man called Moon (the source of her pen name), by whom she had a daughter. But that liaison was no more enduring than the first and she was on her way again. This time she gravitated towards Hollywood and became a script-writer, gaining fame for such films as *Mr Wu*, starring Lon Chaney, and working with directors like Cecil B. de Mille. It was in 1929 that she wrote *Dark Star*, a deeply moving novel about her beloved Buchan but one which appalled the local populace by describing some folk of the Strichen district with unmistakable clarity. Among them was Billy Fraser, described in the book, in the way he was in real life, as a man of stunted growth who was the local librarian. Ignoring the fact that a girl from their own backyard had written a literary masterpiece, Strichen folk fumed with rage, by which time Lorna Moon was well established in America.

Her own father had been outraged by her previous book of short stories, *Doorways in Drumorty*, in which he recognized himself (from a period of working in Africa) as the man who left his family struggling at home while he lived in some style abroad.

To lessen the embarrassment of Billy Fraser, who was still alive at the time, the local library committee decided not to stock Lorna Moon, and that situation persisted throughout Bob Bandeen's years as librarian. But old Charlie Low did ask if he would accept *Dark Star* and *Doorways in Drumorty* as gifts, and Bob readily accepted and lent them privately to those who were especially interested.

When David Toulmin wanted to reissue Lorna Moon's books with Gourdas House, the Aberdeen publishers, he went in search of copies and it was evidently Bob Bandeen who produced them.

Her *Dark Star* had no sooner appeared in 1929 than Lorna Moon was dying of consumption, a woman in her prime at barely forty-four, possessed of that delicate beauty which so often accompanied tuberculosis. By then her fame in America was such that newspapers carried regular bulletins about her health. When she died in Albuquerque, New Mexico, in 1930 they brought her ashes home to be scattered on Mormond Hill, in accordance with her dying wish, and that story became one of the local legends which enlivened my childhood. Strichen had indeed produced a novelist of world class, whatever offence might have been taken at the way she highlighted local foibles.

As a bizarre postscript to that sad tale, my father-in-law, Nelson Keith, was passing Charlie Low's house one day when he found him cementing the doorstep.

'Man, that's a gey fancy troch ye've got, Charlie,' said Nelson Keith.

'Oh ay,' said Charlie. 'It's the boxie they brocht Nora's ashes hame in!'

There is another postscript to this strange story, offering further proof that we live in a funny old world. Into the village of Strichen in 1984 came an American gent whose presence turned a few inquisitive heads, especially when it became known that his surname was de Mille. Word went round that he was a son of the famous Cecil B., Hollywood creator of such Biblical epics as *Samson and Delilah* and *The Ten Commandments*.

Richard de Mille was accompanied on this very personal mission by David Clark, a medical sociologist at Aberdeen Royal Infirmary who was living on a croft at New Deer at the time and who had been engaged by de Mille to undertake research on the background of his mother. The name of his mother? Lorna Moon. During his visit, Richard de Mille was saying nothing about the identity of his father and, when I later wrote to him in California seeking confirmation of his parentage, he wrote back to say: 'I am currently writing in an autobiographical vein and I hope to prepare a volume about Lorna, which will answer the questions you have asked. I do not expect to have a manuscript for several years. In the meantime I think it would be prudent not to discuss details of the story . . .'

He had also written to David Toulmin pointing out that he holds the rights to Lorna Moon's two well-known books. And there, for the moment, this intriguing story must rest.

Bob Bandeen was delighted with the modern interest in the work of Lorna Moon, just as he was delighted to be enjoying the privilege of being alive that day we met at The Cloisters. Among his five children, he too had produced some rare talents, including a brilliant son Robert, who went to work for ICI, and a daughter, Alicia, who followed the missionary trail to the Mary Slessor Hospital in Africa and was feared lost in the Nigerian troubles of some years ago. Happily she survived to become health visitor at Aboyne, on Royal Deeside, while another daughter, Irene, was similarly engaged in her home village of Strichen.

Since our joyous meeting that day, when we took people and places through hand in a well-worn Buchan tradition, Bob Bandeen has passed on to higher plains, taking with him the guarantee that there will be laughter unlimited even in the dullest corners of Heaven. His last words to me were by way of a thanksgiving for the fact that he managed to find something new to celebrate on every morning of his life. Each day was a new adventure, a fresh cause for joy in the experience of this rugged Buchan individualist. Can you think of a better philosophy with which to face the daily darg?

CHAPTER NINETEEN

Gold and Silver

There is an unusual story behind the common bond which I share with a Dutch schoolmaster, Hans Tuyman by name, who was growing up in Holland as a boy of exactly the same age as myself, no more aware of a Scottish village called Maud than I would have known about his native town of Flushing.

While we were lamenting the black-out and food rationing, the absence of oranges, melons, bananas and Cow Candy, Hans had something more serious to worry about, when the innocence of his childhood was invaded by the German armies, storming towards the English Channel to complete their occupation of Western Europe.

To a youngster on the plains of Buchan there was full compensation for the deprivations when a more friendly invasion of soldiers came to occupy our village halls and hotel. We ran from our local school that October day of 1942, filled with excitement as the caterpillar tracks of bren-gun carriers and lorry-loads of the King's Own Scottish Borderers came thundering upon our quiet village of 500 souls and trebled the population within an hour. They had come to prepare for the Second Front which was on everyone's lips, the inevitable attempt to regain a foothold on the European soil from which we had been unceremoniously driven into the waters of Dunkirk in 1940.

The wider strategy of their presence was of less importance to the child mind than the fact that they brought their parades and pipe bands, their swinging kilts and flying maces. It was the stuff of schoolboy dreams as I marched alongside them, the self-appointed mascot, lengthening my stride on tiring route marches, worshipping those big, friendly Borderers like the heroes they were soon to become – and accepting the tuition of that legendary Kelso piper, Jock Gray, who turned me into a fair little player before he disappeared on the road to D-Day.

The KOSB inspired a new level of life in our sober little village of Maud, as well as bringing us our one and only royal visitor, the Duchess of Gloucester (their colonel-in-chief then as now), to inspect her troops and meet the village folk who were inviting them into their homes and providing a canteen in the Pleasure Park Pavilion. In the nearby woods of Brucklay that evening, the military band played Franz Lehár's 'Gold and Silver' waltz, a haunting melody which filtered through the trees to the lazy village below, a scene of blissful serenity in marked contrast to the war which was raging outby. That melody invaded my tender soul and has lived there ever since. For I knew, in the still of that April evening, that here was one of those precious moments in life to distil and to store away for ever, before time untethers it and casts away the fragrance. I knew too that my Border heroes would soon be gone, off to the uncertainties of a war which grown-up people said, in tones of doom, would last for ten years.

When the dreaded day came, I filed in and marched alongside as the whole village turned out to bid a fond farewell. Seeds of friendship and some of love had been sown by these men who now marched off to their next billet at Hayton Camp, Aberdeen, on that route which would take them, step by step, to the south coast of England. Several miles on, they fell out for a rest and Jock Gray put a hand on my shoulder and turned me back, lest my mother was worried.

There I stood, biting a silent lip and fighting back the tears as my heroes went off to war, that vision of the rhythmic mass now blurring like a mirage and leaving me alone to nurse a broken heart. While that heart marched onwards, the rest of me came back to a village now ringing with the hollow sound of a place deserted, the involuntary gasp of a sigh suggesting that life might never be the same again. Mercifully in this wonderful world, the healing property of the broken heart is one of nature's daily miracles.

Long after the Second World War was over and my surviving heroes came home to the mill towns of the Scottish Borders, they began to invite me to their annual reunions – and I have been going there periodically ever since. They are now past the stage of their fortieth anniversary dinner, but when I join them in the Town Hall of Hawick on an October night it is the custom to say a few words, and there, as I rise to face their elderly ranks, I can still feel that hot sting in my throat, as if it were 1942 all over again.

But we laugh and sing and drink together and damned near cry as well. Some come along with wives they met along the way, people like our own Peggy Ellis from Maud, who lived at the West Lodge of Brucklay Castle, where her father was on the staff, before marrying big Alex McLean on his way to France.

One of the most moving aspects of those memorial evenings in Hawick is the presence of a party from Holland and Belgium, people who never fail to come all that distance to reiterate their gratitude to the men who freed them from that Nazi tyranny one day in 1944.

That was how I came to meet Hans Tuyman, the Dutch schoolmaster who was my counterpart in the town of Flushing. Just as I had seen them off to the liberation of Europe from our little community in Scotland, so did young Hans welcome them at the other end of their mission as the men of the King's Own Scottish Borderers went storming ashore at Flushing. To heighten the drama of that evening at Hawick, Hans Tuyman brought with him not only his heartfelt gratitude but some amateur cine-film which showed the actual landing of those men from Hawick and Selkirk and Galashiels and many miles around. From behind the backs of the Germans you could see them advancing to meet the defence. Flushing people, shooting with cameras instead of guns, were recording a piece of priceless, historic film of their liberators' arrival, all the more natural for the mediocrity of its quality.

As we watched in rapt attention, I was conscious of a poignant moment for the man who sat beside me. The stocky frame of Ken Rust gripped the arm of his wheelchair, looked down at his legless body and told me: 'That's where it happened – as we landed there at the docks.' As those Borderers charged ashore, a burst of German gunfire blew off most of Ken's right

leg. With remarkable courage, he grabbed a knife and cut away
the part which still hung loose. So they put him on a stretcher
and were rushing him for treatment, the white flag flying, when
another burst of fire got his left leg. And there we were, seeing
the mayhem at the very moment it happened.

But Ken doesn't complain. From the standpoint of two short
stumps he gives us all a lesson in getting on with life and
making the best of it. As an Englishman who now lives in
Folkestone, he never misses a reunion in Hawick and regards
his Scottish connection with bursting pride when you might
expect that he would want to forget it. Between times, he
hurtles over to the Continent to see that they are looking after
the graves of those who were even less fortunate than himself.
As they all agree, Ken is one helluva fellow and none pays him
greater tribute than Brigadier Frank Coutts, a young KOSB
officer when I knew him in Maud but later Colonel of the
Regiment, a Scottish international rugby player and joint secretary of the Earl Haig Fund and the British Legion, Scotland.

It was Frank Coutts who drew my attention to the brevity of
contact with those Dutch and Belgian people who were liberated
by the Scots. While the Borderers had spent seven months in our
Aberdeenshire village, they met those Continentals for only a
matter of hours on a particular day of 1944. There was no time to
linger for pleasantries when the Hun had still to be defeated. But
they did pick up the names of people like Adri Van Wyngen, an
Underground worker who sped them on their way to victory.
Adri comes back to speak at Hawick, as a result of those very few
hours in which he forged bonds which would last for ever.

Back home in Holland and Belgium they tend the graves and
tell the children about the courageous Scottish soldiers who
came to save the lives of their forefathers. Where windmills
tilt, they are determined that they should never forget those
men. Enjoying the glorious good humour of the heroic Ken Rust
and watching as he happily propels himself in his wheelchair,
I know why I must wear my Flanders poppy on Armistice Day
each year, as a symbol of a debt that can never be repaid.

CHAPTER TWENTY

---◦◦◦---

A Spurt of Oil

Drive down that final sweep from the south into the city of Aberdeen and the glint of grey granite in the morning sunlight confirms that here is one of the most beautiful places on God's earth.

Shielded from a wicked world in its Grampian cocoon, this northern citadel has long maintained a sturdy independence which gave it a distinctive character when so much else of society had slithered down the drain of uniformity. Aberdeen and its agricultural hinterland went their own determined way, riving at a grudging soil, hewing a desirable stone and facing stormy seas to bring home the harvest of the sea. In the process, they moulded their own nature, fashioned their own standards and honed their own dry, biting sense of humour.

But who would have guessed there was oil? All the shrewdness of the Aberdonian became no more than a plaything of fate as she suddenly revealed that a fortune of liquid gold had been lying beneath the offshore doorstop for seventy-five million years or more, leaving the affronted native to call out 'We didna ken, we didna ken.' But they damned well ken noo. If it took foreigners to charm the elusive lubricant from the bowels of the North Sea, the locals were not slow to cotton on to a technology which soon brought them unprecedented wealth.

Millionaires became numerous as Aberdeen floated off on a tide of affluence, heady from the experience and prepared to let the ebb take care of itself.

It is always hard to come to terms with a zenith of history but there is little doubt that, through 1,000 years of Aberdeen, the city reached an all-time peak of experience in that period from the mid-seventies to the mid-eighties, throbbing with a prosperity as the oil capital of Europe which brought no fewer than 50,000 jobs related to that one industry.

But how did it all begin? The historian seeking to pinpoint the first signs of an oil industry in the North Sea would probably find his way to the desk of Ted Strachan, a former colleague of mine on the *Press and Journal* who, when short of a story one day in the sixties, pursued a vague reference to what might possibly lie under the sea bed. And there he produced for his newspaper the very first hint of what could be in store.

Another who remembered the early vibrations was Lord Kirkhill who, as plain John Smith, was a year ahead of me at Robert Gordon's College but was a Labour Lord Provost of the city by the time I talked to him about the coming of oil. He recalled it like this: 'During the sixties I had known geologists who told me there was oil but what they did not know was whether or not its extraction would be commercially viable.'

Big oil companies play their hands close to the chest, but soon there were courtesy knocks on the Lord Provost's door; Shell came to say they had established an office in the old tramcar depot at North Esplanade West; British Petroleum was heading towards a discovery in the Forties Field. Lord Kirkhill's excitement at what was about to break over Aberdeen and the North-East was not shared by all his colleagues on the Town Council, many of whom suffered from Labour's traditional distrust of big business.

'Some felt that big international companies would be in and out for a quick buck, exploiting local people in the process,' said Lord Kirkhill. 'Indeed there are still people in Aberdeen today who don't consider the discovery of oil as of great consequence to the over-all well-being of the city. They think it puts an over-reliance on the relatively easy way of making money and that there will be greater unemployment in the long run. My attitude was to accept the prosperity while it was there; any problem beyond that would be something for our grandchildren to solve. Without doubt this is the most important thing that has happened to our city this century; just as it was granite last century, it is oil in this one.'

By the first stirrings of that oil industry I had long since left for the south, but I suppose I was a natural choice of Beaverbrook newspapers to go back and report on what I found on my native heath.

I headed first for the Cromarty Firth and the shelter of Nigg Bay, where they were scooping out a dock in which they would build the first gigantic oil platform to be towed out to the Forties Field, off the North-East coast of Scotland. From there I drove along the Moray Firth coast by Elgin, Banff, Fraserburgh and Peterhead to the village of Cruden Bay, a golfing resort once sporting a swanky railway hotel like a lesser Gleneagles, which was served by a branch line from Ellon, on the Buchan route of the London and North-Eastern Railway Company.

It was there we used to picnic on warm summer days and ponder the blood-curdling fact that we were on the same spot where the Irish writer, Bram Stoker, used to come visiting when he was creating his horror tales of Dracula. Now it was oil, not blood, they were planning to suck from the depths of the great North Sea, and farmer Jimmy Cantlay had sold fifty acres of Nether Broadmuir which was earmarked as the gathering point for the oil that would gush ashore from its seabed pipe before starting another remarkable journey to the BP refinery at Grangemouth, 140 miles away.

On one of my early despatches to the *Daily Express* in 1971 I wrote:

The whole vibrating atmosphere of a prosperity just round the corner is there to be absorbed in Aberdeen, whether you are walking down the grey granite splendour of Union Street, breathing in the fishy smell of Market Street, joining in the football enthusiasm of Pittodrie Park or relaxing with a pint in a cocktail bar.

Aberdeen has never been a dull city. But now, apart from its own lively social life, with an abundance of cinemas, dance halls, pub entertainment and concerts, the present week's diversions include the Stanley Baxter Show at His Majesty's and Dickie Henderson's All-Star Show, not to mention the regular draw of the roulette tables at the Blue Chip, the Cheval or the Maverick.

Even before the promise of oil, Aberdeen's unemployment was running at only 3.6 per cent, against the Scottish average of 6.3. As the regional capital, it has always been more of a servicing than an industrial centre, a hub of financial operation which includes an incredible total of nearly two hundred insurance offices. But, with a population of 180,000, it had slipped below Dundee to become the fourth city in Scotland, a situation which will soon be reversed.

As to how long the bonanza will last, Lord Provost John Smith says: 'People guess at all kinds of figures but we are assured by the oil companies that, whatever the final outcome, there is twenty-five or thirty years of production lying out there in the Forties. So we see it as a matter of continuing job opportunity. The marine servicing industry, for example, will play an increasing role with renewal work. Light industry is bound to benefit from what they now call spin-off work. The hotels, restaurants and pubs as well as the whole food and drinks industry will benefit.'

Outside, as the November sunlight catches the grey granite from the spires of Marischal College right uptown to the posh dwellings of Queen's Road and Rubislaw Den, the tangible signs of oil begin to mushroom.

One telling sign was the decision of British European Airways to move the headquarters of its entire helicopter service from Gatwick to Aberdeen Airport because of the volume of work now involved in carrying personnel to and from oil rigs and bases. Around the local folklore names like Fittie and Point Law and up by Old Torry to Girdleness, the wider names like 'Global' and 'Transcontinental' appear on modest shore bases, announcing that the big oil men are here to probe but do not wish to make too much noise about it until they are sure the liquid is gonna gush.

Crowds gather to gaze at the rig-ship in port, while divers and roughnecks of sundry nationality come and go in a buzz of activity.

Across in Torry you will find a long, lean Texan, name of Calvin Seidensticker, draping himself over a desk and drawling words like 'gee' and 'mighty fine' into a telephone. Actually things are not so fine as they might have been for Mr Seidensticker. As drilling supervisor for Mobil exploration in Aberdeen, he says 'Yeah, I guess you could say we are a little disappointed that we have not so far found oil. It has been costing us £10,000 a day but we are not giving up . . .'

Other companies, like British Petroleum, have found oil all right and it is now mainly a question of how many of the giants strike it lucky enough to make a final decision to go ahead.

Not everyone in Aberdeen wants oil. There are fishermen who fear it will alter the eating habits of the fish as well as provide difficulty for their nets. There are sectional business interests which don't particularly relish the rising demand on harbour accommodation, nor the rising level of wages that an oil bonanza will bring.

But these are minor considerations. Aberdeen is on the march as the centre of a prosperity which will stretch right down the east coast from Orkney to Dundee and beyond.

So there is oil and business and finance and research; there is still a substantial fishing industry as well as papermaking and granite and a vast agricultural hinterland creating its own industrial structure.

Inevitably there are the camp followers, the women whose nose for an opportunity is as sure as their profession is old. Taxi-drivers are already well versed on the habits and the hang-outs, whether they be in downtown dockland bars or the more plush surroundings of a West End cocktail bar.

One luscious lady from London was reporting that she was doing business in Aberdeen which surpassed her achievements in the metropolis. And her pad is not in a seamy backstreet but in a swanky Deeside suburb where ladies play golf and bridge and raise teacups with pinky held high. All part of the business of prospecting for prosperity, I suppose, the only difference being that, unlike the ladies of easy virtue, Aberdeen has been sitting primly on a fortune all those years – and didn't know it!

Thus I recorded the growing excitement about oil in the North-East of Scotland in 1971.

CHAPTER TWENTY-ONE

A Royal Day

Away out there in the Forties Field, 110 miles off the Aberdeen-shire coast, a vast reservoir of oil lay awaiting the suction pumps of mankind, several miles beneath the bed of the sea and trapped in impervious layers of rock. It lay not in wells of liquid, as one normally imagined, but rather like water to be extracted from a sponge, marine organisms transforming into gas and oil over that unthinkable period of millions of years.

At last the human race was coming to fetch it as a modern fuel to sustain the circus of civilization, with a technology to baffle the most fertile imagination. Mankind would not only have to build those giant platforms (each one with nearly as much steel as the Forth Railway Bridge) and tow them out to an angry reception from the most inhospitable of waters, but it would also be necessary to drill towards the furnaces of hell to a depth which, if taken upwards instead of downwards, would reach the summit of Mont Blanc in the Alps. Then there would be the pipeline covering hundreds of miles along the seabed to find land at Cruden Bay and continue down the subterranean route to Grangemouth.

Those miracles of technology, perhaps the greatest engineer-ing feat in the story of mankind, were duly completed over the four years from my earlier visit to the North-East, and it was for a very special occasion that the *Daily Express* sent me back to Aberdeenshire on Monday, 3 November 1975.

This was my report of an historic day, not only for my native part of Scotland but for the whole British economy:

What a glorious occasion it was – a Royal occasion, a Scottish occasion, blessed with sunshine and colour and the atmosphere of a gala celebration. It was the day when Britain became an oil-producing nation.

The presence of Her Majesty the Queen and the Prime Minister [Harold Wilson], his Cabinet colleagues and a thousand invited guests suddenly crystallized the distant myth of North Sea oil into a living reality. Here at the village of Dyce, on the outskirts of Aberdeen, we were witnessing the creation of that chapter of history which will tell our grandchildren of the new industrial revolution.

From all the talk and argument and barrage of statistics it now came clear, even to the least technically minded, that the miracle had worked. The oil was flowing from the silent depths of the North Sea bed, a hundred miles east of Peterhead, ashore to the Scottish coast and south to the BP refinery at Grangemouth, all symbolized by the pressing of a button by the Queen. Here we were, marking a memorable event with one of the biggest sprees ever seen in Scotland, costing British Petroleum somewhere around £700,000. But what was that compared to the £745 million it has already cost the company to bring the oil ashore?

It was all in sharp contrast to the pastoral scene twenty-five miles to the north of this Royal occasion – at Cruden Bay, where the great pipeline comes rising out of the North Sea like a monster from the depths of hell. The oil which had lain there for seventy-five million years or more was being sucked from that sponge-like substance below the seabed of the Forties Field and, as it struck land at Hay Farm, Cruden Bay, there was hardly a hint of this great day in Britain's history. For the pipe goes almost immediately underground, buried in the fields of farmer Geordie Carnie, who has already grown and harvested a crop of oats on the restored soil. Yesterday he went off to plough his stubble field, little aware of the golden wealth which flowed under his feet on its way to the lubrication of the national economy. 'I'll jist ploo awa,' said Geordie. 'I dinna expect the Queen will bother comin oot this wye.'

Significantly perhaps, the pipeline comes ashore in the political constituency of East Aberdeenshire, a Tory stronghold until last year but now part of that North-East shoulder of Buchan, Banff and the Moray coast which has gone solidly over to Scottish Nationalism. Douglas Henderson, the Nationalist Member for East Aberdeenshire, was at Dyce yesterday declaring to all who would listen that this was a great day for 'Scotland's oil'. Undoubtedly Mr Henderson and the people of his constituency, whose close contact with the activity of oil has sharpened their awareness of the new-found wealth, echo a broader cry across Scotland for a greater say in the running of their own affairs.

Today, however, the oil and the running of Scotland belonged to Westminster, symbolized by the full array of first-team members, making it plain to those who had any doubts about the matter that this was a British occasion.

Mr Wilson was here to greet the Queen and speak about this milestone in Britain's economic history. Mr Callaghan, the Foreign Secretary, and Mr Benn, the Energy Minister, were here and so was Mr Ross, the Scottish Secretary, and his Tory predecessor, Lord Campbell of Croy, the Liberal leader, Jeremy Thorpe, the Nationalist chairman, Willie Wolfe, Shadow Energy Minister Patrick Jenkin, Reginald Maudling and so on.

Aberdeen had never seen a gathering like it. Whoever owns the oil, the main function of this day was to rejoice in the fact that it was flowing in quantities which would soon reach 400,000 barrels per day, a statistic which can be meaningless until you calculate that each barrel carries nearly forty gallons. (This field alone will provide a quarter of Britain's oil needs.)

So we rejoiced in a £48,000 tent which was reminiscent of Bertram Mills Circus, with its dais of radiant red and muted blue, with concealed television sets to show the spectators what they might be missing in the flesh.

Television's Donny B. MacLeod compered the show and jollied the audience into a warm-up session before the Queen arrived.

The Grampian Police pipe band skirled a real Scottish welcome and the regimental band of the Gordon Highlanders, flown home specially from Singapore, were given a heroes' reception in the land where they belong.

Then came the Queen in emerald green, serene and thoughtful, turning to face the audience as they joined in the National Anthem. Prince Philip looked on tenderly and Prince Andrew stood straight as a guardsman. Among those presented to Her Majesty was Mr Matt Linning, the engineer who masterminded the North Sea operation. The Royal Family met other BP workers and walked out among the flag-waving children from local schools before the Queen moved into the main BP operations centre from which the whole flow of oil from the Forties Field is controlled.

There she pressed the button which inaugurated, with ridiculous simplicity, a whole new age for Britain. We awoke from the technological dream and finally accepted the fact that it was all for real. The battle to wrest the liquid gold from the vaults of nature had been won against heavy odds. 'Oil Strike North' was no longer just a series on television; as from this moment, Britain was now an oil-producing country, its citizens the blue-eyed Arabs of North-West Europe.

In the words of Her Majesty, it was a story of excitement and romance. And, as she drove out of the tented arena on her way to the nearby airport, the crowd rose and cheered, waved and rejoiced. The band struck up 'God Save the Queen'. In such a setting of historic splendour, it would have been a hard man who did not have a lump in his throat.

Less than three years later the Queen was back on the Buchan coast, some miles further north, to perform a similar ceremony for the arrival of gas. That took place at the unpretentious village of St Fergus, where nothing very much had ever happened before, though the district gained its name from an early Christian preacher who is said to have wrought miracles in the Buchan area. As far as we know, the creation of gas was not one of them.

CHAPTER TWENTY-TWO

◆

Golden Age of Aberdeen

The modern romance of oil, with all its reputed gains and losses, was not readily discernible on the face of Aberdeen as I returned to the granite canyon of Union Street in the 1980s, seeking proof that extraordinary things had been happening these last ten years.

Exiles like myself could still find the reassurance of familiar landmarks. Robert Burns, as ever pigeon-encrusted, still brooded in Union Terrace while the mighty sword of William Wallace remained poised in a gesture of unjustifiable threat towards the magnificence of His Majesty's Theatre. Floodlit spires still rose like Northern Lights in the deepening melancholy of an evening sky.

The native tongue, as heard in city restaurants, was little different from days gone by, except for an occasional slickness of phrase and the alien ring as it curled round subjects once unheard of: 'Ach, I dinna like praans wi ma avocado!'

But the veneer was so thin you could be tempted to think the North-East was much the same place as it was in my childhood, when we came stumping in from rural Buchan to savour the excitements of city life. I could still re-create the adrenalin of the young boy arriving from our village of Maud to be schooled at Robert Gordon's College.

Bombs may have been falling in the wartime black-out but tramcars still clanked their way up a Union Street bustling with crowds in their utility coats; a scent of coffee still wafted from Collie's delicatessen; and the dreichness of a grey day could soon be forgotten in the celluloid magic of the picture houses.

On this sentimental journey of mine there was still a lingering image of broth and butteries, though no longer an Isaac

Benzies in George Street in which to sample them. It was only when you ventured up Albyn Place and Queen's Road that you began to notice those miniature palaces of residence now converted into offices. Great blocks of headquarters proclaiming the names of Conoco, Marathon or Britoil stood on the edge of the old Rubislaw Quarry, that legendary hole in the ground just off Queen's Road, from which the bulk of Aberdeen's grey granite was hewn.

Driving out to Altens or the Bridge of Don you would find industrial estates where once the contented cow would chew her cud. Walking down by the harbour of an evening you marvelled at the floodlit spectacle of ships with names like *Seismic Explorer, Cromarty Service, Lido Supplier.* Mosey into one of the plush hotels and hairy roustabouts with names like Rick and Chuck were mighty glad to meet you, sir. There too you could be subtly propositioned by that new breed of sophisticate who operated discreetly, in contrast to the old-fashioned Aberdeen whore who plied her trade overtly along the harbour area.

Any suggestion of a red-light district, however, was without foundation, a fact of the oil boom which bewildered a visiting investigative reporter from Fleet Street who refused to believe that a major oil capital could be so lacking in immoral purpose.

Piece by piece, the modern reality of Aberdeen began to dawn. A gnawing sense of having missed out crept over the exile, a feeling of coming home and finding that a stranger has been enjoying too well the hospitality of your house. Not all, of course, were strangers. Charles Skene, who took our wedding photographs as a member of the family which owned Studio Morgan, had long since wearied of arranging bridal groups and had turned instead to property, a major investor with his base in Queen's Gardens, an address at which three of his adjoining properties had a market value of nearly a million pounds. That was typical of what had happened to the housing market in Aberdeen as a result of the inflationary effect of an oil boom. As a young journalist I had stayed in lodgings just off Carden Place, a pleasant enough suburban street but not in the top bracket of residential properties in the city. Yet houses costing £5,000 in 1964 were changing hands for an unthinkable £250,000 by 1984, popular with companies which converted them into offices and were drawn by the spacious front gardens which became valuable as private car-parking spaces.

Inevitably, the housing market created its own problems. Though average wages in Aberdeen were high, the modest artisan was struggling to survive and companies were finding it difficult to recruit from other parts of the country because of the gap between home-selling prices elsewhere and buying prices in Aberdeen.

Business men, complaining of high rates, were not all prospering from oil. Retailers were feeling the pinch and even hotels, apparently well cushioned by the block bookings of oil companies, were running into trouble with loan interest. The plush American-style Huntly Hotel and the Victoria (formerly the Douglas, where we used to dance on Saturday nights to Fred Cowie and his orchestra) were among companies to land in the hands of the receiver. By 1986 the rush of bankruptcies and list of unsellable houses had reached alarming proportions, in the wake of falling oil prices – and just as the prophets of doom had forewarned – but long before that, Aberdeen had spawned its own new breed of multi-millionaires, leaping like the salmon of the nearby River Ythan.

From my own village of Maud, young George Simpson, the joiner's son, had moved to Aberdeen to be a draughtsman when oil arrived, deciding to take a mortgage on a flat instead of paying for lodgings. He then saw the prospect of buying for let another flat, and another, self-financing projects which soon turned modest little George into the boss of his own multi-million property company, Kildonan Investments of Queen's Road.

The most dramatic story of all the entrepreneurs, perhaps, belonged to another man in his early forties, Ian Wood, son of a ship-repairing family who turned away from a brilliant academic career to pick up his business heritage and extend it into the age of oil. While most local business people seeking a share of the new prosperity had contented themselves with a servicing role, lucrative enough in itself, Ian Wood joined the big international brigade of people who actually drilled and produced the oil.

The result was an overturn of £90 million, with 2,300 employees and a type of business which could be taken wherever they were drilling around the world, long after the North Sea days were over.

Wood had shown himself to be a young man with the insight of a visionary, anxious to take advantage of the heaven-sent opportunities of oil yet never losing sight of the indigenous industries which would one day be called upon again to provide a living for the North-East of Scotland. He harboured a secret fear that his grandchildren might look upon his generation as the one which took the benefits to themselves and failed to preserve the heritage.

Not everyone made the millions of a Wood or a Simpson or countless others, but there were also more modest stories of enterprise which warmed the heart of the returning exile. I met Denny Morrice and his wife, Margaret, who ran a little newsagent's shop in Thistle Street. Seeking his own crumb of comfort from the oil boom, the jovial Denny went knocking on the doors of big oil companies offering to supply newspapers to the men on the rigs. Happily, they responded to his enterprise and Denny soon found himself heading for the wholesaler's depot at 4 a.m. with a number of assistants, bringing back the papers to the wee shop in Thistle Street and preparing them in bundles to be delivered to the helicopters at Aberdeen Airport. With just a little bit of thought, life had never been so sweet for Denny and Margaret Morrice.

Into the fabric of local life had come whole communities of itinerant oilmen and their families, to the extent that there were both a French and an American school in Aberdeen. Accustomed to exploring in less civilized surroundings, these people had a history of depending on themselves, which had rather come apart in the North-East of Scotland. Though they still held their own house parties, with bridge a favourite pastime, the Americans had integrated with local life so well that one of their sons became school captain of Robert Gordon's College.

As I wandered on through the back ways I turned into Exchange Street and was faced by an illuminated sign on a pub which proclaimed 'Willie Miller's', a reminder that all was not oil in Aberdeen. Was it indeed a coincidence that the high mark of the city's history had run parallel with a similar peak in the football fortunes, of which the illustrious name of Willie Miller, greatest player and captain in the entire history of Aberdeen Football Club, was a shining symbol?

Blossoming within that period of oil, Aberdeen FC had succeeded in doing what all others had failed to achieve during the whole of the twentieth century, namely breaking the tiresome monopoly of the two Glasgow giants of Scottish football, Rangers and Celtic. The Dons became the dominant force in Scottish football from the late seventies to the mid-eighties, carrying all before them, even to the point of becoming the top team in Europe in 1983, when they not only beat the legendary Real Madrid for the European Cup Winners' Cup, but clinched the honour by beating Hamburg in the final of the European Super Cup.

The late Chris Anderson, that fine innovator of football ideas who played for the club before becoming its vice-chairman, refused to separate that success from the presence of oil. It had given the whole city a new belief in itself, he claimed. Taking a cue from the Americans, local people walked tall as Texans in their new-found confidence.

Side by side with oil and football, I concluded, there had been a curious upswing in cultural fortunes, as if fate were getting its act together. The industrial prosperity had undoubtedly brought a new awareness of North-East Scotland, which had so often been by-passed by the touring public in favour of more rugged wilderness to the west. There were minor matters, like David Puttnam discovering the picturesque hamlet of Pennan, near Fraserburgh, as a location for filming *Local Hero*, starring Burt Lancaster. But even before the focus came fully upon

Aberdeen and its hinterland, there was already a pattern of fate developing in tandem with oil.

In that watershed year of 1970 the BBC finally released the distinctive dialect of Aberdeenshire on the nation's network through the televised version of Grassic Gibbon's novels, which were found to be intelligible even in the United States. So there followed the works of Jessie Kesson and James Duthie and suddenly Aberdeen found there was a renaissance of local culture and a new level of acceptance in the outside world, where the life and the speech of the area were now more freely understood.

Within the same period, that rare phenomenon of satirical entertainment, which questions the bravado of 'Scotland the Brave' by calling itself 'Scotland the What?', had spread its fame throughout the world; while that other form of entertainment, television's Jim and George of the BBC's *Beechgrove Garden*, also played its part in focussing attention on an area long regarded as eccentrically apart.

On this pilgrimage to Aberdeenshire I found myself caught up in local festivals of poetry, music and drama, with more youngsters capable of playing a fine tune on the fiddle than could ever have been said of my own day. And if the new recognition needed an international ambassador, it materialized in the form of Annie Lennox, a North-East girl who not only became the world's greatest female Rock star of the eighties but never forgot to come back and see her granny, Mrs Dora Ferguson in Maud!

On reflection, this renaissance of culture may well have sprung from an instinctive fear that alien forces were insidiously at work and that local tradition had better be re-defined and preserved before it was too late.

So you could walk down the length of Union Street in the age of oil and sense the pride and prosperity of it all. There were bigger cars, well-stocked shops and plush hotels serving sophisticated dishes where once the Aberdonians would have contented themselves with a plate of stovies or skirlie or mince and tatties.

Grassic Gibbon used to complain of a certain bleakness in the Aberdonian character but his short life was devoted to that early part of this century which included the First World War, the poverty of the twenties and Depression of the early thirties. If only he could have accompanied me on that walk down Union Street in the eighties I think he would have tempered his assessment with elements like confidence and buoyancy, perhaps at times a shade of arrogance.

I concluded this particular part of the pilgrimage with an evening walk and came upon the old Tivoli Theatre in Guild Street, down by the Joint Station, suddenly remembering that I had taken Charlie Chaplin on a nostalgic visit to the Tivoli in 1970 (yes, that watershed year again). By then the boom of burlesque had long since given way to the call of 'Bingo!' but the scent of a bygone day still lingered in doorway signs which said 'Grand Circle' and 'Fauteuils Stalls'. Chaplin had recalled for me vividly his early days when he came to Aberdeen as a boy to clown with Fred Karno. We were already a world away from the baggy pants of a legendary clown but, as we looked back to some good old days, who could have guessed in 1970 that better ones lay ahead? How could we possibly have known that the Golden Age of Aberdeen was lurking round the corner?

CHAPTER TWENTY-THREE

Granite City Growl

If Aberdeen was riding on a zenith of historical experience, affluent and vibrant as never before, it was not everyone who took a favourable view of its current state. Indeed there were inevitably criticisms which were valid and which had already been freely voiced.

None of that, however, prepared Aberdonians for the assault which came their way on the morning of 7 August 1983, when those who opened the *Sunday Times* were confronted with an article by the distinguished American writer, Paul Theroux, in which he poured out the most vitriolic verbiage on the subject of Aberdeen. Mr Theroux, who had written in most entertaining fashion about many parts of the world, had been living in London for ten years without ever venturing outwards to Wales or Scotland or even to many parts of England you might have expected him to have visited.

Suddenly he tired of London and set out on a whistle-stop tour of Britain, which would result not just in a series of articles but in a full-scale book, called *The Kingdom by the Sea*, from which the *Sunday Times* was printing extracts. Mr Theroux's declared hate of Aberdeen would have been bad enough in the transience of a morning paper, but to give it a hardback permanence which would be read by an international audience for years to come seemed like a gross injustice to the North-East.

Of course Mr Theroux was entitled to his opinion (our native humour makes us fairly tolerant of those who fail to discern our intrinsic worth!), but a writer of his reputation was under some obligation to seek out the other side of the story. That newspaper extract infuriated many people, including myself, and I immediately phoned Frank Giles, editor of the *Sunday*

Times, to ask for the right of reply on behalf of my fellow-Aberdonians. That was duly granted, and my article appeared in the *Sunday Times* on the following week, under the headline of 'Granite City Growl'. With the permission of Mr Theroux's agents, I am now quoting that part of *The Kingdom by the Sea* which applied to Aberdeen, followed by the text of my own response. Mr Theroux had travelled from Glasgow up the west coast to Cape Wrath and down to Inverness. From there he came by train to Aberdeen and this, in his own words, is what he found during his fleeting visit:

We reached the coast. Offshore, a four-legged oil-rig looked like a mechanical sea monster defaecating in shallow water. It was like a symbol of this part of Scotland. Aberdeen was the most prosperous city on the British coast. It had the healthiest finances, the brightest future, the cleanest buildings, the briskest traders. But that was not the whole of it. I came to hate Aberdeen more than any other place I saw. Yes, yes, the streets were clean; but it was an awful city.

Perhaps it had been made awful and was not naturally that way. It had certainly been affected by the influx of money and foreigners. I guessed that in the face of such an onslaught the Aberdonians had found protection and solace by retreating into the most unbearable Scottish stereotypes. It was only in Aberdeen that I saw kilts and eightsome reels and the sort of tartan tight-fistedness that made me think of the average Aberdonian as a person who would gladly pick a halfpenny out of a dunghill with his teeth.

Most British cities were plagued by unemployed people. Aberdeen was plagued by workers. It made me think that work created more stress in a city than unemployment. At any rate, this sort of work. The oil industry had the peculiar social disadvantage of being almost entirely manned by young single men with no hobbies. The city was swamped with them. They were lonely. They prowled twilit streets in groups, miserably looking for something to do. They were far away from home. They were like soldiers in a strange place. There was nothing for them to do in Aberdeen but drink. I had the impression that the Aberdonians hated and feared them.

These men had seen worse places. Was there in the whole world an oil-producing country that was easy-going and economical? 'You should see Kuwait,' a welder told me, 'you should see Qatar.' For such a man Aberdeen was civilization. It was better than suffering on an oil-rig a hundred miles offshore. And everyone who had been in the Persian Gulf had presumably learned to do without a red-light district. Apart from drinking and dancing Scottish reels there was not a single healthy vice available in Aberdeen.

It had all the extortionate high prices of a boom town but none of the compensating vulgarity. It was a cold, stony-faced city. It did not even look prosperous. That was some measure of the city's mean spirit – its wealth remained hidden. It looked over-cautious, unwelcoming and smug, and a bit overweight like a rich uncle in dull sensible clothes, smelling of mildew and ledgers, who keeps his wealth in an iron chest in the basement. The windows and doors of Aberdeen were especially solid and unyielding; it was a city of barred windows and burglar alarms, of hasps and padlocks and Scottish nightmares.

The boom town soon discovers that it is possible to make money out of nothing. It was true of the Klondike where, because women were scarce, hags came to regard themselves as great beauties and demanded gold dust for their grunting favours; in Saudi Arabia today a gallon of water costs more than a gallon of motor oil. In Aberdeen it was hotel rooms. The Station Hotel, a dreary place on the dockside road across from the railway station, charged £48 a night for a single room, which was more than its equivalent would have cost at The Plaza in New York City. Most of the other hotels charged between £25 and £35 a night, and the rooms did not have toilets. I went from place to place with a sense of mounting incredulity, for the amazing thing was not the high prices or their sleazy condition but rather the fact that there were no spare rooms.

For £25 I found a hotel room that was like a jail cell, narrow and dark, with a dim light fifteen feet high on the ceiling. There was no bathroom. The bed was the size of a camp cot. Perhaps if I had just spent three months on an oil rig I would not have noticed how dismal it was. But I had been in other parts of Scotland, where they did things differently, and I knew I was being fleeced.

To cheer myself up I decided to go out of the town. I found a joint called 'Happy Valley' – loud music and screams. I thought: Just the ticket.

But the doorman blocked my path and said, 'Sorry, you can't go in.'

Behind him were jumping people and the occasional splash of breaking glass.

'You've not got a jacket and tie,' he said.

I could not believe this. I looked past him into the pandemonium.

'There's a man in there with no shirt,' I said.

'You'll have to go, mate.'

I suspected that it was my oily hiker's shoes that he really objected to, and I hated him for it.

I said, 'At least I'm wearing a shirt.'

He made a monkey noise and shortened his neck. 'I'm telling you for the last time.'

'Okay, I'm going. I just want to say one thing,' I said, 'You're wearing one of the ugliest neckties I've ever seen in my life.'

Up the street another joint was advertising 'Country and Western Night'. I hurried up the stairs, towards the fiddling.

'Ye canna go in,' the doorman said. 'It's too full.'

'I see people going in,' I said. They were drifting past me.

'And we're closing in a wee munnit.'

I said, 'I don't mind.'

'And you're wearing blue jeans,' he said.

'And you're wearing a wrinkled jacket,' I said. 'And what's that, a gravy stain?'

'Ye canna wear blue jeans here. Regulations.'

'Are you serious? I can't wear blue jeans to an evening of country and western music?'

'Ye canna.'

I said, 'How do you know I'm not Willie Nelson?'

He jabbed me hard with his stubby finger and said, 'You're nae Wullie Nullson, now piss off!'

And so I began to think that Aberdeen was not my kind of place. But was it anybody's kind of place? It was fully-employed and tidy and virtuous, but it was just as bad as any of the poverty-stricken places I had seen – worse, really, because it had no excuses. The food was disgusting, the hotels over-priced and indifferent, the spit-and-sawdust pubs were full of drunken and bad-tempered men – well, who wouldn't be bad-tempered? And it was not merely that it was expensive and dull; much worse was its selfishness. Again it was the boom town ego. Nothing else mattered but its municipal affairs. The newspapers ignored the Israeli invasion of Lebanon and the United Nations' initiative on the Falklands and the new Space Shuttle. Instead, their headlines concentrated on the local money-making stuff – the new industries, the North Sea Pipeline about to be laid, the latest oil-rigs. The world hardly existed, but financial news, used cars and property took up seven pages of the daily paper.

The *Aberdeen American*, a fortnightly paper, had the self-conscious gusto of a church newsletter. It was a hotch-potch of news about barbecues, schools, American primary elections and features with an Ango-American connection. It was a reminder that the American community in Aberdeen was large. The American School had three premises. I heard American voices on the buses. And I was certain that it was the Americans who patronized the new health clubs – weight-loss emporiums and gymnasiums with wall-to-wall carpets. A lovely granite church had been gutted and turned into 'The Nautilus Total Fitness Centre'.

On a quiet street in the western part of the city was The American Foodstore. I went there out of curiosity, wondering what sort of food Americans viewed as essential to their well-being on this savage shore. My findings were: Crisco, Thousand Island Dressing, Skippy Peanut Butter, Cheerios, Pepperidge Farm Frozen Blueberry Muffins, Bama Brand Grape Jelly, Mama's Frozen Pizza, Swanson's Frozen Turkey TV Dinner, Chef Boyardee Spaghetti Sauce, El Paso Taco Sauce and Vermont Pancake Syrup. I also noted stacks of Charmin Toilet Paper, Budweiser Beer and twenty-five pound bags of Purina Dog Chow.

None of it was good food and it was all vastly inferior to the food obtained locally, which cost less than half as much. But my experience of Aberdeen had shown me that foreigners were treated with suspicion, and it was quite understandable that there was a sense of solidarity to be had from being brand-loyal. Crisco and Skippy were part of being an American – and, in the end, so was Charmin Toilet Paper. I imagined that, to an American in Aberdeen, imported frozen pizza was more than cultural necessity – it was also a form of revenge.

'Isn't there *anything* you like about Aberdeen?' Mr Muir asked imploringly, as we waited on the platform at Guild Street Station for the train to Dundee. I had spent ten minutes enumerating my objections, and I had finished by saying that I never wanted to see another boom town again. What about the Cathedral, the University, the Museum – hadn't I thought the world of them?

'No,' I said.

He looked appalled.

I said, 'But I liked the bakeries. The fresh fish. The cheese.'

'The bakeries,' Mr Muir said sadly.

I did not go on. He thought there was something wrong with me. But what I liked in Aberdeen was what I liked

145

generally in Britain; the bread, the fish, the cheese, the flower gardens, the apples, the clouds, the newspapers, the beer, the woollen cloth, the radio programmes, the parks, the Indian restaurants and amateur dramatics, the postal service, the fresh vegetables, the trains, and the modesty and truthfulness of people. And I liked the way Aberdeen's streets were frequently full of seagulls.

Under that heading of 'Granite City Growl', the *Sunday Times* carried my reply, as follows, in the following week's edition:

Whatever it lacked in Christian charity, if Paul Theroux's Epistle to the Aberdonians had been no more than the provocative prose of a passing journalist, it might have been dismissed for its transparent shallowness. But Mr Theroux has presumed to write a permanent record, which will spread across the world an impression of Aberdeen and Aberdonians which does, at the very least, beg correction.

An 'awful city' which he came to hate? Stony-faced, smug and unwelcoming and not even offering the compensation of vulgarity? Dear dear.

There is, of course, a strong element of impertinence in passing through a strange place, snatching at a few random experiences and coming up with a snap judgement which some might mistake for responsible study.

Let me give you another side of Aberdeen, through the eyes of someone who has regularly returned to his native corner of Aberdeenshire to conclude that the Granite City remains one of the truly civilized cities in the world.

Imperfections? No city which becomes the oil capital of Europe can escape the scars of prosperity. Where there's oil there tends to be a veneer of vulgarity, loud bar talk from a set of roustabouts more intent upon cocktail chrome and hovering whore than local culture.

And culture is there in abundance. Aberdeen, city of fish and flowers and good humour, is currently on an upswing of local writing and music, not to boast about its art gallery, concerts and theatre which Mr Theroux failed miserably to unearth. For those who insist on pursuing the sweaty disco, an encounter with a clutch of Kentucky dudes should come as no surprise.

Seek further, Mr Theroux, and you will find an Aberdeen inextricably bound up with its rural hinterland, a race of those same honest, hard-working and independent folk who so impressed you on the wilds of Cape Wrath.

While sheep and resignation continued to rule in the bareness of the Highlands, the Aberdonians got down to transforming a sour and grudging soil into a land of high production, turning out the best of British beef, with oats to make the porridge and barley to fill the whisky vats.

A dozen generations have bent their backs in an agricultural conversion which ranks with the greatest achievements of mankind. Such drudgery in an inhospitable climate may have left them short of time to develop superficial courtesies but it brought them many a useful trait instead.

In a Grampian cocoon they move with the gait of their beloved Clydesdales, slow to impress or flatter yet sure and loyal when friendship has been earned. Clearly Mr Theroux did not linger long enough to find out.

He could have learned too about their dry, piercing humour, expressed with an economy of words and typified in the tale of the English commercial traveller, arriving early for his train and placing his umbrella and briefcase on a seat before retiring to the buffet.

When he returned the carriage was filled with ruddy Aberdeenshire farmers going home from market and deeply engrossed in their short-stemmed pipes. 'Excuse me, gentlemen,' said the traveller, 'but when one puts one's umbrella and briefcase on a seat it rather indicates that one has reserved that seat ... at least in the part of the world where I come from.'

Whereupon one rosy farmer piped up: 'Ah weel, my mannie, in this pairt o' the world, it's erses that coont!'

Here then, Mr Theroux, is no sunny California of swimming pools and nasal brats with too much money and too little discipline. But need we apologize for it? Here is a breed of worthwhile men and women, the like of whom you will find in your own American land, in places like North Dakota, where I have downed a soothing dram with toothless cowboys who still conclude big cattle deals by the old Scots custom of slapping the hand, declaring that a man's word is his bond.

Such men had never been in New York or Los Angeles and were appalled that I might judge their great country by the human assortment I might find there. To those fine American people, these cities seemed like the most God-awful holes in Christendom. I wouldn't have gone that far, not even about the soulless wastes of Detroit which, now that Mr Theroux tempts me, might well lay claim to some of his extravagances about Aberdeen.

There is one final treat I would have reserved for Mr Theroux had I been able to steer him around this northern citadel. In Britain's first all-seated, all-covered stadium, he could have sampled the delights of a football team, new champions of Europe, whose skills might have stirred his aesthetic instincts.

These are not, of course, your great lumbering hulks with padded shoulders and steel helmets where their heads ought to be, but men of balletic artistry.

If such delicacies were not too far removed from the din of disco Mr Theroux would surely, given time, have begun to understand the subtlety of it all.

CHAPTER TWENTY-FOUR

—◆◈◆—

The Auld Hoose

On a winter's day not so long ago I drove, from the south, through a snowstorm which would certainly make me late for a very important dinner at the New Marcliffe Hotel in Aberdeen. In treacherous road conditions, vehicles were being abandoned by the roadside and the car radio was bringing me police reports of no fewer than fifty accidents in the stretch between Glasgow and Stirling, a situation which filled me with anxiety.

Good manners dictated that I should arrive on time for this auspicious occasion, all the more so since the Gordonian Association, the former pupils of Robert Gordon's College, had invited me to be their Guest of Honour and principal speaker: Gordonian of the Year, 1986! What would they have called me in 1946? The irony of the situation helped to divert me from the chaos of the road conditions. For was it not exactly forty years ago that I had walked out through the vaulted gateway of Gordon's College in Schoolhill, Aberdeen, with the tears of remorse streaming down my cheeks, the ring of failure resounding in my ears? Would Gordonians now recognize the pale-faced lad of fourteen, nervously going home to face an irate father in Maud with nothing much more to show for three years of academic misadventure than the certificate of a shattered confidence?

In retrospect, it seemed far too tender an age for any human being to be set on the motorway of life in such a state of depression. Yet too many good things had happened since then to leave any balance of bitterness.

Despite serious illness, which followed very soon, I had recovered in time to carve a reasonable niche of my own and there was still room in my heart for a reservoir of good feeling about the Auld Hoose. The beginnings had been quite promising. On the May morning of that entrance examination in 1943, as I arrived from Maud with the odd straw sticking out of my lugs, a smart young city lad came forward on the steps of the MacRobert Hall and offered to relieve my mother of the burden. He would see that I was all right. That was the start of a friendship with Stanley Shivas, as suave and debonair at eleven as he was later to be known in his role as a distinguished journalist, indulging himself in the casinos and caverns of nocturnal opulence, in the service of those who read the *Daily Record.*

In his longing to peer beyond the drystane dykes of Buchan, the shy loon from Maud had regarded a glimpse of the swimming pool at Tarlair or the boating pond at the Cooper Park in Elgin as symbols of a more glamorous world outby. Now he was joining the throng in the big city of Aberdeen which, though essentially an agricultural market town with an odour of fish, seemed to the innocent mind to have all the deliciously wicked trappings of a cosmopolitan centre.

As I settled into digs with Miss Stott at 14, Elm Place, I was vaguely conscious that this majestic city of grey eminence had already wound itself into the fabric of my emotional being. Was it not here, at Kittybrewster, that my father would unload us from our little Austin motor on Friday mart days, during the school holidays, to join a tram-car down George Street towards 'The Queen' at Union Street?

That excitement of a day in town would be rounded off with an hour in the Astoria Cinema before returning to the car-park at the mart, where the withered gypsy face of Madame Veitch, in her caravan by the corner, stirred the trembles of mystery in the child breast.

Was it not here, in the faded pink of a June evening in 1940, that I stood on the beach esplanade and gazed with a queer mixture of emotion towards the south where, for the purposes of my imagination at least, a distant rumbling brought eerie echoes of the Dunkirk evacuation and filled me with a sense of narrowly missing out on the action of history? We had just had a happy day attending my Aunt Betty's wedding in the

Palace Hotel and rounding off the occasion with a visit to Harry Gordon's show at his famous Beach Pavilion on the promenade.

Then we drove home the twenty-eight miles to Maud, out by the double-road at Bridge of Don and on to Balmedie, Ellon and Auchnagatt, back to an uneasy co-existence with 200 evacuee children from the Dowanhill and Hyndland Schools of Glasgow, with whom we would plod to Maud School, complete with gas-masks over our shoulders, and find excitement in the periodic air-raid drills when we would dash home in response to the dominie's whistle. The dominie was Donald Murray, who had come to Maud School in 1937, having been headmaster at Skene, where he made such an impression on an orphan child called Jessie Kesson that she later dedicated to him her memorable book *The White Bird Passes*, with that quotation from R. L. Stevenson:

> Bright is the ring of words
> When the right man rings them
> And the maid remembers

Donald Murray, who used to regale us with great tales of meeting Lord Baden-Powell when a young Boy Scout, conducted the kind of local school which made Scotland famous for its education; yet the exquisite nature of my seven years there did not reveal itself until much later. How strange it is to look back on childhood and find that the actual number of years involved seem far too few to embrace the wealth of compacted experience which lingers with you for the rest of your life. Either time has played a clever trick, or the child mind, in its response to new experience, has absorbed and lent importance to an inordinate amount of detail.

Whatever the case, in the midst of that war to end all wars I was moving to Aberdeen, where the emergency was heightened by the existence of an air-raid shelter in Elm Place, into which we all crowded one fearful night when the German bombers came bumbling over like angry bees. There were air-raid shelters, too, in the fore-lawns of Gordon's College, bringing overtones of twentieth-century warfare to the very place where

Butcher Cumberland stationed his troops on the way north to Culloden and again on his victorious way home.

His plundering soldiers were billeted right there in the main building of the school, in those ancient rooms up well-worn stairs, where people like Long Tom made brave attempts to teach us mathematics. When that lofty gentleman lost his temper and brought down the leather strap from a great height, you could have sworn that some of Cumberland's aggression had affected him.

Long Tom came to school on a double-barred bicycle, upon which he balanced in a most precarious fashion, and it was the special joy of pupils to greet him with the obligatory salute and to watch as he tried to return the courtesy while wobbling with only one hand on the handlebars.

Boys were always boys, sometimes to cruel effect, as in the case of another teacher of mathematics, known as Knockers, a kindly and sensitive man who had been shell-shocked in the First World War as I remember, and who could be goaded into a frothing fury when boys would blockade his room or pay an organ-grinder to play in the lane beneath his classroom window. The poor man collapsed and died in the staff-room on the first morning of the new session, 1945–6, perhaps unable to face another year of torment and leaving many a Gordonian with a hint of conscience about his part in the destruction of a fine human being.

So there was an array of notable personalities on the teaching staff of Gordon's College, saddled with such names as Fat Bill, Hooter, Frosty, Pudner, Johnny Mac and Greasy Bob. Many of the able-bodied were away to war, which increased the scope for women, some of whom had been there since the similar emergency of the First World War. With a warm irreverence we called them Moosie, Squeezy, Bunty and Skinny Liz, spinster ladies of a lost generation, dedicated teachers who epitomized that fondness for sound education which gave the North-East of Scotland the highest adult literacy rate in all Britain during Victorian times.

To a wide-eyed innocent from the country, however, that

road to literacy stood little chance against the bright lights which beckoned from every corner. For educational purposes we had been taken to hear Sir John Barbirolli and the Hallé Orchestra at the Music Hall and to see Shakespearians like Donald Wolfit playing Shylock in *The Merchant of Venice.* I had already had the privilege of hearing the incomparable Richard Tauber at His Majesty's, that gem of theatrical creation designed by Frank Matcham in 1906, during the reign of King Edward VII, and would later revel in the peerless repertory of the Wilson Barrett Company and the Whatmore Players. They brought every notable performer of the day, from Stewart Granger (earning £10 a week, I have discovered) to Michael Denison and his wife, Dulcie Gray, alternating with grand opera, ballet, pantomime and the summer seasons of every Scots comedian from Dave Willis to Rikki Fulton.

At the matinée performances in His Majesty's I used to be intrigued by the fact that you could be served with afternoon tea, brought to your seat if you were in the Orchestra Stalls, the Parterre Stalls or Dress Circle. After that, I have discovered, Jimmy Donald ran short of cups! I was just as likely, however, to be found in the less salubrious setting of the Tivoli Theatre in Guild Street, where vaudeville survived and you were liable to be entertained by a mixture of trick cyclists, bawdy comics, dancing girls in fish-net stockings and a boy soprano who went on for so many years and became so broad in the hips that dark rumour suggested he might well be a soprano but had never been a real boy!

On light evenings I would be found at Linksfield Stadium, just off King Street, supporting the St Clement's football team which included a dashing right-winger called Martin Buchan, who would later father a son of the same name to captain both Aberdeen and Manchester United in the respective Cup Finals of Scotland and England, the only footballer ever to do so.

After school on a Friday I would buy my *Evening Express* from Patsy Gallacher at the corner of Union Street and Union Terrace and head down Bridge Street towards the Joint Station, past the site of the Palace Hotel, which had been burned down in 1941, the year after we had attended my aunt's wedding.

Back home in Maud at weekends I would play the drums in my Uncle Gavin's dance band for ten shillings a night, touring the village halls and having my eyes opened by an adult world where men away at war were sometimes replaced in their wives' affections by passing soldiers. The child mind was quick to sense the liaisons, even as I caressed the brushes round my little drum to the beat of our signature tune, which was 'All the World is Waiting for the Sunrise', symbolizing perhaps our yearning for a youth now sadly stunted by Hitler's holocaust. When that monster finally perished in his Berlin bunker we lit the bonfires of Victory-in-Europe Night, 8 May 1945, and waited for the sunrise of a brave new world. Somehow it was all too late for the flowering of a proper teenage, and the world we saw, when the lights went up again, stood poor comparison with the childhood memory of the 1930s.

Despite its Depression, that earlier decade still beckoned like a golden glow as it filtered through the hideous ruins of the Second World War and came to torment us on the other side. Winston Churchill, architect of victory, came driving up Union Street in an open car that April day of 1946 to receive the acclaim of an electorate which had already, paradoxically, consigned him to the Opposition benches. That seemed to me like foul ingratitude as I ran alongside his car and reached out to touch him, with cries of 'Good old Winnie!' In the same week I was innocently making my stage début on the boards of that same MacRobert Hall where I had sat the entrance examination, now playing a minor role in *The Auld Hoose*, the story of Robert Gordon and his college.

I still have the programme, which shows that I was engaged in a scene with a certain contemporary called William D. Hardie, taking his own first steps towards fame on the stage under the name of Buff Hardie, a contraction of his childhood nickname which was 'Buffalo Bill'. A brilliant student, Buff not only went on to mastermind the student shows at Aberdeen University but gained a scholarship to Cambridge in those satirical days when Jonathan Miller had just gone and Peter

Cook was soon to arrive. Returning to Aberdeen, where he later became Secretary of the Grampian Health Board, he teamed up with two other student performers, Stephen Robertson, who had become a city solicitor, and George Donald from Huntly, a schoolmaster who was to become deputy headmaster of Perth Academy. Performing through the 1960s, they decided to devote more time to their young families and planned a farewell appearance at the Edinburgh Festival of 1969.

There they were seen by Neville Garden, then a colleague of mine on the *Scottish Daily Express* (he was related to the famous Aberdeen opera singer, Mary Garden), who wrote that this was the funniest show at the festival. The crowds flocked in and, instead of a farewell, those three Aberdonians who called themselves 'Scotland the What?' found that their career was just beginning. By public demand they extended their appearances from Aberdeen as far as London's West End and from stage shows to records and cassettes. Their name became legendary in a role which could be described as a modern satirical extension of the mood portrayed by the great Aberdeen comedian Harry Gordon, with a humour rooted every bit as firmly in their native culture. By the 1980s, in the prime of middle age, they gave up their secure and well-paid careers to cast themselves into the more precarious but also more lucrative realm of full-time show business, three delightfully natural and humorous men whose friendship I have long enjoyed.

So these were some of the thoughts which occupied my mind as I ploughed through a snowstorm on the way to the Gordonian dinner in Aberdeen. Fortunately the weather improved the further north I drove and the company was just finishing its meal when I breezed breathlessly in to snatch at the main course before facing the most important audience of my life.

Just twenty-four hours earlier I had seen my Honeyneuk film beaten on a casting vote for the Special Programme prize at the Television Awards and now, in rather inauspicious circumstances, I was gathering my thoughts and trying to unjangle the nerves for a speech which needed to go some way towards disproving the events of forty years earlier. After a eulogy from the distinguished psychiatrist, Dr Robert Davidson of Glasgow, I rose to respond. Burdened with a stammer, I could never claim public speaking as one of my strengths but there are moments in life when the Lord comes suddenly on your side. After the turmoil of a troubled day, anxiety drained miraculously out of my system and I spoke for twenty-five minutes without a written note or a moment of hesitation. I knew what I wanted to say and said it. By my own mediocre standards, it was by far the best speech I have ever made. The Auld Hoose, which had despatched me from its vaulted gateway with a heavy heart in 1946, had welcomed me back into the fold, the academic failure now acclaimed for whatever he had made of himself.

It was a night of revelry extending from hotel to the Queen's Road home of the president, Ian Edward, where I rounded off a rather important occasion in my life with a company which included those good friends, Steve Robertson and the same Buff Hardie with whom I had shared that theatrical stage oh so many years ago.

CHAPTER TWENTY-FIVE

—◆◆—

The Queen and John Brown

Deeside looked just as serene and beautiful as Queen Victoria always said it did when I drove westward to Braemar and Glenshee beyond. Indeed the old Queen herself was much in my thoughts as the spectacle of her beloved Aberdeenshire home came closer, mile by mile, and the intriguing question of her association with John Brown, the Balmoral manservant, began to engage my mind.

It was a perfect springtime day on which to follow the silver thread of the river as it wove its picturesque pattern through a valley of rich foliage. At Dinnet, just forty miles from Aberdeen, a granite slab was telling me that I was 'now in the Highlands', which seemed to me like a bit of a liberty. I can never imagine my native county as having much in common with the Highlands since Aberdeen itself is such a lowland city in character and outlook. Surely there is more to the Highlands than high lands. It is a whole separate culture and language, stretching down the western half of Scotland as far as Glasgow and Argyll and quite distinctly different from the North-East corner. Soon I had reached Ballater, where Dark Lochnagar frowned down disapprovingly from its lofty perch, white-capped and haloed in a ring of spring cloud.

So I sped on past Balmoral and drew in for lunch at the Inver Hotel, where Jack Crawford was dispensing beer with bonhomie and his wife, Frances, cooked Sunday lunches in the heat of the kitchen.

While her skill in the creation of a steak pie delighted my palate, it was her other claim to fame which occupied our discussion. When Jack took over the burned-out shell of the old Inver Inn and set about re-constructing it in the seventies, Frances opened up in business as a hairdresser to eke out the

157

family living. With an old shed at the back as her salon, there was nothing more basic to be found in all the land, nothing further removed from the high coiffure of London fashion. Imagine, then, the surprise when the telephone rang one day with a call from Miss MacDonald, a lady-in-waiting to the Queen. She was calling with a royal request: that Mrs Crawford should come to Balmoral to do the Queen's hair! Once she had recovered from disbelief, the homely Mrs Crawford left the confines of her portable shed and drove across the River Dee to the majesty of Balmoral Castle en route to her first royal appointment.

'On that first occasion I was so nervous that, when I came back, I could only remember seeing the figure of the Queen,' she told me. 'I could not have told you what was in the room or anything else I saw.'

But the result of her efforts must have been just fine because Frances Crawford has since become Her Majesty's regular hairdresser when she comes north. Promptly at 3.45 on a Wednesday, a chauffeur picks her up and drives her the three miles to Balmoral where she enwraps Her Majesty in a gown like any other customer in a salon, tilts the head of the Head of State over the basin and gives her a good old wash-and-set.

'I am still nervous on the first visit each year,' Frances told me, 'but the Queen soon puts me at ease and after that I really look forward to the weekly visit. I wait for Her Majesty to lead the conversation. When Princess Grace of Monaco was killed, for example, she spoke about the tragedy and I could see that she knew her very well and was most upset about it.'

On another tragic day, Frances was present when the Queen opened up to her on the assassination of Lord Mountbatten, on whom she laid such store. Far away from the uncertainties of London, the Queen is very much at home with the folks of Deeside, who are the solid, dependable salt of the earth so beloved by Queen Victoria.

'She knows all that is going on in the district,' said Frances Crawford whose father was a blacksmith on Deeside, called in on occasion to shoe the horses at Balmoral. 'When my husband was rebuilding the hotel from a burned-out shell, she knew all about it. On the day of Braemar Gathering last year I was outside with a coachload of people who had been having their afternoon tea here, when the Royal car came past on the way to the Gathering. The Queen spotted me and waved, much to the delight of the day trippers. I feel I know her better now and she seems more relaxed with me. We are invited to the annual Ghillies Ball and what a lovely atmosphere there is in the ballroom, with Charles and Di there and the Queen Mother dancing away as usual.'

Jack and Frances Crawford have recently left the Inver but have remained in Crathie, from which the royal hair appointment is still kept every Wednesday.

As I was saying, the mystery of Queen Victoria's connection with John Brown had been occupying my mind on that Deeside adventure, heightened by an evening I once spent with Elizabeth Byrd, the American authoress who based herself in Edinburgh and was so fascinated by the subject that she wrote a historical novel about it.

In Victoria's own day, the magazines went as far as to report (quite daringly for the period) that the Queen and her manservant were secretly married and that she had gone abroad to have Brown's baby. The reports were nonsense but Victoria's own reaction to the baby story was merely to laugh. To say the least of it, she was indiscreet in her connection with John Brown and, according to Elizabeth Byrd, she was almost certainly in love with him.

John Brown's father was schoolmaster at Crathie, near Balmoral, and the basic facts of the story are that the teenage Brown, who was eight years younger than the Queen, was a stableman at Balmoral, even before Victoria bought it. He became a ghillie and a great favourite of Prince Albert, who asked him to lead the Queen's pony when they went on their safaris into the hills. John Brown was a tall, good-looking man with red beard and hypnotic eyes, according to all reports, and Victoria herself became very fond of him.

But there was nothing untoward in their relationship until

after Albert's death in 1861, when the Queen was in her early forties. She then appointed him her personal attendant, on constant call, and gradually their association became much more intimate, according to Miss Byrd. The evidence apparently is that, when the Queen went to pieces and began the long mourning, John Brown had to lift her from couch to bed and back again; he was in and out of her room without knocking and could sit down in her presence and smoke and even drink if he liked – and he did. He was a heavy drinker and taught the Queen to drink whisky.

John Brown seems to have accompanied Queen Victoria everywhere, including tours abroad, becoming devoted and protecting her from all that bored her, including her own family and the Prime Minister of the day, William Ewart Gladstone, whom she never liked. There was an evening at Balmoral when Brown, who was honest, sincere but very blunt, was standing behind the Queen at dinner as Gladstone was going on and on about something. He could see clearly that she was bored and that some action had to be taken, so he tapped the Prime Minister on the shoulder and said sternly 'That's enough, that's enough!' The great Gladstone had to shut up.

This is how Miss Byrd answered my question about the actual evidence of Queen Victoria's love for John Brown:

> When a woman loves a man, she cannot stop talking about him. And Victoria talked a great deal about him in her leaves. When Brown died at Windsor in 1883, at the age of fifty-six, nobody could bring himself to tell her. The shock paralysed her legs and for days she would not see anyone or put her signature to anything.
>
> She even wanted to write a biography of John Brown but was finally dissuaded by the Dean of Windsor. She also wanted to publish his diaries but was persuaded to have them destroyed.

Whether or not the affair was sexually consummated is likely to remain a mystery for ever. Though Victoria was prim, pious and prudish in some respects she was also regarded as a very passionate woman sexually and is said to have worn out poor Albert, who did not exactly relish his role as royal stud.

No love was lost between Brown and Victoria's son Bertie, later to be King Edward VII. In fact the future king loathed the servant's bluntness. One day, it is said, he came into Balmoral demanding to see his mother but Brown told him she was having her nap. When the Prince insisted, he was told in no uncertain manner what to do with himself!

After Victoria's death, he destroyed almost every statue and cairn the Queen had raised for Brown but did not dare tamper with the loving inscription which she had placed on his gravestone at Crathie churchyard. It spoke of 'that friend on whose fidelity you count, that friend given you by circumstances over which you have no control. This stone is erected in affectionate and grateful remembrance of John Brown, the devoted, faithful personal attendant of Queen Victoria, in whose service he has been for 34 years . . . enter thou into the joy of thy Lord.'

There is also a statue to Brown within the grounds of Balmoral Castle, lauding him as friend more than servant, loyal and brave. He was born at Crathie on 8 December 1826 and died at Windsor on 27 March 1883.

From the widespread researches of Elizabeth Byrd Victoria seemed to emerge as more of a red-blooded being than her stony portraits suggest. She used to appal titled ladies by encouraging the tradition of the ghillies ball at Balmoral, where they had to dance with 'uncouth, sweaty, drunken servants'.

It is perhaps a measure of the lady who reigned for those sixty glorious years that such earthy experience did nothing to blunt the feminine appetites which evidently burned so fiercely beneath those skirted folds.

CHAPTER TWENTY-SIX

The Mighty Monty

That old winding gramophone which skraiched in protest under the heavy metal of a muscular arm and needed a new needle for every record was our symbol of modern entertainment before the Second World War.

You could go to the pictures at Peterhead or tune into the wireless, which were other novelties of that decade, but there was a special excitement about hauling out the heavy box from under the bed, setting it upon the kitchen table and cranking it up in anticipation of the first selection. With the sentimentalist's weakness for hoarding, I still have many of those old records which spun round at seventy-eight revolutions per minute under the Beltona label and cost half-a-crown, which translates into twelve-and-a-half pence in modern language, a greater proportion of a wage-packet in the thirties than a long-player would cost today; and you were getting only seven or eight minutes for your money.

The records we turned out in those innocent days had titles like 'Red Sails in the Sunset', Will Fyffe's 'I Belong to Glasgow' and 'I'm 94 Today', as well as our own Harry Gordon's popular songs of the time, 'Hilly's Man', 'I Wish I were Single Again' and 'The Auldest Aiberdonian'. But the mixture also included melodies like 'Trees', played by Henry Hall and his Gleneagles Hotel Band, 'Ave Maria' by John McCormack, 'O sole mio' by Enrico Caruso and 'Drink to Me Only' by Lawrence Tibbett.

While the essential Scottishness of our existence seemed stronger before the war than ever it did afterwards, the music of the time was not given over exclusively to bothy ballads and old Scots songs. The wireless and cinema had made their mark, bringing in the Charleston of the flapper era and the synocopated rhythms of the thirties which fascinated me immensely.

To discover the occasional Lew Stone record among the antiquity of our household collection was always a delight which sent me on my first faltering steps of ballroom dancing.

One of the highlights of those childhood days in Maud was the weekly visit of a continental dancing teacher who lived in Aberdeen, Marguerite Feltges by name, who taught us eurhythmics and introduced us to the modern waltz. Whatever rhythms eluded me in my speech were made good in the body and Miss Feltges wanted to take me under her wing for some professional training. But the rural distance of Maud was not the ideal location for budding Fred Astaires. Browsing through that record collection, I find the changing mood of the times reflected in the appearance of Benny Goodman with 'Lady Be Good', Joe Loss with 'In the Mood' and Glenn Miller with 'Perfidia'.

With the Second World War behind us, it is interesting to see what a teenager of the late forties and early fifties was gathering in his record collection, as the popular tunes of the day, before the blast of Rock 'n' Roll and subsequent events came to change the face of contemporary music, not to mention the pattern of human behaviour itself.

Far from adhering to the uniformity and slavish dictates of puppeteers in London, my collection ranged from the orchestras of Harry Roy and André Kostelanetz, Cyril Stapleton and Victor Sylvester to the solo arpeggios of the incomparable Freddie Gardiner and his mellow saxophone and the warmth of Steve Conway's crooning. In covers marked 'Jack Webster, 2 Park Crescent, Maud, 25th September, 1947', I still have 'J'attendrai' sung by Tino Rossi, 'La Ronde' by Anton Wallbrook, 'A Beggar in Love' by Guy Mitchell, followed by 'Island in the Sun' from Harry Belafonte and 'In a Shady Nook' by Donald Peers. In the affections of an Aberdeenshire teenager in that post-war period, however, there was also room for a full range of music from Ivor Novello, George Gershwin, Richard Rodgers and singers like Richard Tauber. Heaven preserve us, there was even a place for the tenor tones of Jimmy Young.

Just as our musical horizons had expanded, there was an

increasing movement of people, not that the Scots were ever lacking in enterprise when it came to turning up in distant parts. Two of my father's aunts, Sophie and Babs Watson, had been typical of the young Scots girls who went south at the turn of the century to provide the service of the aristocratic households of England. With a high standard of expectation ingrained in their very nature, they served as cooks to people like Admiral Beatty, hero of the Battle of Jutland in 1916, and the Cayzer shipping family, in stately homes where the guests would include King Edward VII.

Sophie would come home to Buchan to tell us great tales of her service in the London home of a prominent Egyptian, whose handsome young son was completing his English education by chasing maids around the house. That apprenticeship in hedonism was later to produce a bloated monarch affectionately remembered by dear old Sophie as the young King Farouk of Egypt. Good advice from influential employers enabled these thrifty Scots lasses to invest their wages in valuable stocks, and long before they retired, Sophie and Babs had established a home in Stanmore, Middlesex, to which they could repair in their time off. That home, in which those truly gentle spinster ladies eventually settled, also became my London base when I first went south to explore the excitements of the metropolis, laden with butter and cheese and oatcakes and anything my mother could produce to remind them of home.

On at least one occasion during those visits the dutiful grand-nephew would take the ladies to the West End to see an Ivor Novello musical, and there they would recall bygone days in the theatreland of London, giving me a fine sense of the atmosphere in Edwardian times.

In 1949 I was merely passing through London en route to Paris for the first time, boarding the express for Newhaven and Dieppe and savouring a flavour of the French capital which still lingered from pre-war days. It was not so long ago that jack-booted Nazis had goose-stepped down this same Champs Élysées but now the lights were bright once more, the *Folies Bergère* was restored to former glory, with Josephine Baker to entertain, the Lido had opened up again and Montmartre was beckoning with all the lurid promise of a naughty madame.

Four years later I was back in Paris, this time en route to the Balkans with my journalist friend John Lodge, from the *Press and Journal* in Aberdeen, with whom I was to explore the Communist state of Yugoslavia. We joined the Orient Express at 8.30 on a Saturday night and arrived in Belgrade at the dawn of Monday, cold and hungry and miserable, without a word of the language in a country which was not then geared for tourism. Soon we fled over the Dinaric Alps to the greater warmth of Dubrovnik which, in 1953, did not even have an airport. The old Pionair plane came bumping down on a grazing field where cattle and horses were programmed to scatter for the daily arrival.

In his more liberal way, President Tito had permitted a measure of private enterprise and around the arrival shed women pushed forward young daughters as bait if only we would come to lodge in their homes. In that rather pathetic scene we found a distinguished gent who spoke English and turned out to be the boss of telephones in Dubrovnik. Back at his council house his wife, Dusanka, proved to be an equally distinguished looking lady, a pre-war friend of the king who now found herself in the more straitened circumstances of a Communist regime. In that year of Queen Elizabeth's Coronation, Dubrovnik was not yet a holiday resort for overseas visitors so we explored the ancient, walled city and the modern spread beyond and suddenly found ourselves intrigued by a villa which stood aloof, its lawns sloping down in terraced steps to the waters of the Adriatic below.

'It's the Villa Sheherazade,' they told us, 'where President Tito entertains his foreign guests. Princess Margaret comes there but your war hero ... Field Marshal Montgomery, yes? ... he stays there at present.'

The instinct of two keen young journalists led them to the heavy gates of Villa Sheherazade where we negotiated with an armed guard and left a rather presumptuous request for an interview with Field Marshal Montgomery of Alamein. He would hand it in and deliver the reply if we presented ourselves at his guard-room at 6 o'clock that evening. The tones were perfunctory and far from encouraging.

However, we duly presented ourselves at 6 p.m. for the anticipated rebuff. Instead, the gates of Sheherazade swung open and a military guard ordered us to march this way, down through terraced gardens and trees and fairy-lights and across the lawn to a table in front of the villa. A small figure rose to greet us: 'What can I do for you, gentlemen?'

It was the unmistakable figure of Monty, sitting out in the warm, balmy September evening. We explained our mission and he invited us to join him at the table. Remembering his own teetotal habits, we hesitated over an offer of drinks till he saved us the bother and called for two glasses of vermouth. A man in dark suit arrived with silver tray and handsome glasses and placed them before us. We acknowledged him momentarily; but the 'waiter' who had obeyed Montgomery's instruction then pulled up his chair to join us – and turned out to be none other than M. Popovic, the Yugoslav Foreign Minister!

We may have imagined we were there to interview Montgomery but he used the occasion to question us about our own experiences which lay outwith his own itinerary. How were the people in their own homes? What was the state of the agriculture?

We talked about Alamein and his contacts with Churchill. ('Last weekend, when I was visiting Winston, he was telling me what he was backing in the St Leger'.)

John Lodge and I were then the employees of Lord Kemsley, who owned the vast newspaper empire later to be acquired by Lord Thomson of Fleet, stretching all the way from London to Aberdeen, where Kemsley's daughter married the Marquis of Huntly. As the lights glistened from the trees above on a cascade of waterfalls, Monty showed us out and left us with a parting message: 'Do tell my friend, Lord Kemsley, that I was passing on my regards.'

Did he really mean it? Was it just the kind of thing people say? Lord Kemsley was well beyond the orbit of a couple of juniors but we decided to take no chances. Back in Aberdeen, we rather sheepishly sent him a message with the Field Marshal's regards.

A few days later another message arrived on Lord Kemsley's desk. It was a letter which said:

My Dear Kemsley,

I was in Yugoslavia recently, as you may have seen, and while there I met two young men from the Aberdeen Press of your group, John Lodge and Jack Webster. They asked if they could come and see me and they came to my villa that evening.

I thought they were both extremely nice young men, very courteous and interested in everything. They told me all about their experiences and they had, without doubt, displayed great initiative in making the journey on a limited amount of foreign currency. They gave me the impression of being two very fine types of young journalists, keen and alert, and proud of being in the Kemsley Group. I told them that they were to send you personally my good wishes – and I hope they did so . . .

Montgomery of Alamein

How glad we were that we took the trouble! Whatever else we learned that memorable night, we could now understand more fully the mind of a great soldier in his attention to detail. No wonder he routed Rommel in North Africa.

CHAPTER TWENTY-SEVEN

God Bless America

That encounter with Montgomery of Alamein was the first in a long list of major interviews I was to conduct in the years ahead. Though my career in journalism is not the subject of this book, I should perhaps explain that that was what took me away from the North-East after I had learned my craft as a reporter with the *Turriff Advertiser*, the *Evening Express* and the *Press and Journal*, for whom I was the resident Buchan staff man, based in Peterhead and Fraserburgh between 1951 and 1954.

A move to the *Scottish Daily Express* in Glasgow on Leap Year Night of 1960 was the first step towards a career as a features writer which brought to fruition all the romantic dreams I had ever nursed about being a journalist. Each year became a greater excitement than the last as I found myself in the company of people like Charlie Chaplin, Bob Hope and Bing Crosby, Mohammed Ali and Stanley Matthews, Paul Getty and Sophia Loren, even Margaret Thatcher and the notorious Christine Keeler, with whom I conducted an interview in the not inappropriate setting of a bedroom.

Glancing over the diary of 1972, for example, I find I started the year in Northern Ireland, being caught up in an ambush with an army patrol in the Turf Lodge district of Belfast. By April I was accompanying crippled children in the candle-lit procession of the sick at Lourdes. In May I was shaking off my Russian shadow and roaming freely in the streets of Moscow (only to be apprehended at the airport and questioned about my movements), discovering, among other things, what a potentially capitalist nation the Soviets really are. That summer was spent in Germany and by September I was flying off to Singapore, sampling life in the jungles of Malaya and landing at a party in the company of Princess Margaret. Restoring a sense of unreality to life, I ended the year back in the mayhem of Northern Ireland, where it had all started in January.

Among other experiences of the 1970s, I found myself one day in the London home of Lord Mountbatten, father figure of the British Royal Family, who was giving me what turned out to be a rather poignant interview. The man who fought gallantly in two world wars and took the surrender of the Japanese in 1945 was fighting an even greater battle to bring the youth of the world together. It was an idealistic scheme called the United World Colleges, the brainchild of Kurt Hahn, founder of Gordonstoun School in Morayshire, where Lord Mountbatten's nephew, Prince Philip, was a pupil before sending all three of his sons there. By now Mountbatten was head of the organization and there we sat talking about the future of civilization in general and the role of his favourite grand-nephew, Prince Charles, in particular.

Suddenly he remembered I worked for the newspaper empire of Lord Beaverbrook, a man well known to have a blacklist of public figures. As we relaxed in that London drawing-room, he broke into a smile and told me the story of Anthony Eden, Britain's debonair Foreign Secretary in the days of Churchill and a man high on Beaverbrook's blacklist.

Apparently, when Churchill was standing down and Eden was offered the Premiership in the Spring of 1955, he consulted Mountbatten on the wisdom of accepting, referring in particular to Lord Beaverbrook, whose power in those days could go a long way to making or breaking a politician.

'I'm right at the top of Beaverbrook's shit-list, you know,' he told Mountbatten. 'He'll crucify me.'

'No, you're wrong there, Anthony,' Mountbatten countered. 'I'm the one who heads the Beaver's shit-list!' And from all accounts, he was probably right.

We were able to laugh about it a generation later. What we did not know as we sat in the calm of that London town-house, to which I had been admitted with a minimum of security vetting, was that, much more sinister than being high on Lord

Beaverbrook's shit-list, Mountbatten was also figuring in the IRA's hit-list. During his next annual visit to Classieburn Castle in County Sligo, he was on a family boating trip from Mullaghmore Harbour when an IRA man detonated a planted bomb by remote control. A great man was blown to smithereens, along with three more of his party, including his fourteen-year-old grandson.

Before I leave my journalism of the 1970s, there is some relevance in recalling my assignment in the United States in 1976, when the *Express* sent me to describe how that extraordinary nation was celebrating its 200 years of independence.

This is what I wrote about a rather special Fourth of July, a day when I also renewed acquaintance with a colourful Scots-American who will warrant a later chapter of his own:

They are dancing in the streets of America tonight. The bands are playing, majorettes are marching and the biggest-ever display of fireworks is exploding around the pious head of George Washington on that majestic sweep before the White House.

The Viking spacecraft may be hovering for the final touchdown on Mars, 200 million miles away, but the action for tonight is here on Mother Earth, from New York to San Francisco, from the Custer battlefields of Montana to the jazzbands of New Orleans. For this is the 200th birthday of the most remarkable nation in man's history and they are not going to let it pass unnoticed.

This is America, loud but lovable, of Hollywood and hamburgers, baseball, Bing and Broadway, of Dallas, Deadwood and the Almighty Dollar. It is good old star-spangled, bible-belting, corny-as-Kansas America, baring its soul and seeking to exorcize the nightmare of a devilish decade or more.

And this is the day when you want to embrace it all. Personally, I settled for a drive down from New York to Washington, passing through Philadelphia, where they signed the Declaration of Independence 200 years ago today and cut the American people loose from the apron strings of Mother Britain.

New York had to be seen to be believed. As if by deliberate contrast to the magic of a spacecraft on Mars, this great city surrendered itself to the charms of the windjammers, or tall ships as John Masefield called them.

An armada of 225 sailed up the Hudson River at nature's pace, under the Verazanno Bridge and past the upraised arm of Liberty's Statue, watched by a crowd estimated in millions and including President Ford. A big American beside me threw away his cigar and said, gee, that sure was the most touching sight he had ever seen.

The man with the finest view of all was multi-millionaire Malcolm Forbes, the publisher whose father was a poor country boy from Whitehill in the parish of New Deer, Aberdeenshire.

Mr Forbes's magnificent yacht, the *Highlander*, was berthed in the 79th Street basin and he was holding a party for his distinguished guests, some of America's top business people.

Having sampled the caviar and venison of the Forbes party, I headed for Washington with its history stretching from the original George, who couldn't tell a lie, to the shady men of Watergate, who couldn't tell the difference. In this capital city, which rivals Paris for its wide-avenued splendour, they had come from the morning church services to join in the celebrations. Among the simple words which Thomas Jefferson wrote down in the Declaration of Independence was the fact that everyone had the right to enjoy 'life, liberty and the pursuit of happiness'. And that is a pretty fair description of tonight's activities.

Two hundred years ago these words were tantamount to a kick in the pants for the British but the bitterness of the past had melted in the warmth of friendship. They welcomed the pipes and drums of the Scottish infantry as they beat Retreat tonight at Quantico, outside Washington.

I bumped into Miss Duncan MacDonald, who was preparing to head off to the Scottish Highland Games in North Carolina, which attracts a crowd of 40,000 over two days. Miss MacDonald runs the Scottish-American Heritage body and told me: 'In this age of computerized living we have found that young people in particular are trying to trace their ethnic roots. Those of Scottish descent all want to know what clan they belong to. It is as if they are seeking the strength of personal identity in this anonymous age.'

As the summer winds blew gently down the plains of Oklahoma, the Americans are thus consolidating their past before turning to face a new century. Whatever terrors that may hold are deep in the lap of the gods. It is enough to raise a glass tonight, to join in the singing of 'God Bless America' – and leave the rest to fate.

CHAPTER TWENTY-EIGHT

Fairy-tale of Forbes

Exactly ten years later, the man who welcomed his guests aboard the yacht on that memorable day of American history was stepping up the aisle of the Mitchell Hall at Marischal College, Aberdeen, complete with gown and hood and sustained by a procession of solemn academics.

Malcolm Stevenson Forbes had come back to receive the honorary degree of LLD from Aberdeen University in recognition of his outstanding achievements as publisher, writer and adventurer and one of America's most colourful and influential characters, who owed his origins to the plain, unpretentious land of Buchan.

Somewhere built into that honour was a tacit recognition of his father, the late Bertie Charles Forbes, whose story I recounted in *A Grain of Truth*. Briefly, he was one of the ten children of a poor country tailor at Whitehill of New Deer who became a pupil of my great-grandfather, Gavin Greig, a man he came to idolize. Gavin Greig helped him on the road to a newspaper career, via the *Peterhead Sentinel* and the *Dundee Courier* to the *Rand Daily Mail* in Johannesburg, which he helped to establish with Edgar Wallace, the thriller writer. The financial markets fascinated him and in 1904, at the age of twenty-four, he sailed for New York, passing under the mighty arm of Liberty who called upon the world to 'give me your tired, your poor, your huddled masses, yearning to breathe free'.

Without money, job or influence he soon took the outrageous step of renting a room in the old Waldorf Astoria, for the purpose of gaining proximity to famous men like John D. Rockefeller, Henry Ford and Frank Woolworth. It worked exactly as he had planned and the story of Bertie Forbes has now passed into business legend. Not only did the world's most powerful newspaper owner, William Randolph Hearst, offer him a blank cheque to write his own salary but he started his own business magazine which stands today as the most influential journal of its kind in America.

Appropriately, it is called simply *Forbes*, a fortnightly publication which runs to the length of a novel on most issues, a businessman's bible which lands on 727,000 desks and is reckoned to have one millionaire in every ten of its readers.

Bertie returned to his native corner of Buchan every two years to entertain the local folk to a picnic, bringing his beautiful wife and five sons to stay at the old railway hotel at Cruden Bay. As a great-grandson of Gavin Greig, I gained more than my share of his attention, as if he were repaying a back debt of gratitude. It was there at Cruden Bay during the 1930s that I first remember young Malcolm and his brothers. When Bertie dropped dead at his Manhattan desk in 1954 it was the eldest son, Bruce, who first took over the reins, but he developed cancer and died in his forties, at which point the mantle fell to Malcolm.

After Princeton University and a distinguished war career, in which he was badly wounded at the Normandy landings, his calling seemed to be for politics. In the 1950s he was seen as the Republicans' answer to the up-and-coming John F. Kennedy and was widely tipped as a future President of the United States. A bad defeat for the Governorship of New Jersey ('I was nosed out – by a landslide!' he joked later) gave him second thoughts about politics and diverted him back to the family business in time to take over Bruce's role. By the mid-sixties he was the sole owner and autocratic head of the multi-million enterprise and remains so today, making him something of a rarity in an age of corporations and limited liability.

In his plush headquarters on Fifth Avenue he reigns like a king, entertaining top people at his adjoining town-house or on the fabulous *Highlander* which plies between the Hudson River and Florida. Intimate photographs with people like Presidents Eisenhower, Nixon and Kennedy and the Rockefellers abound, and Malcolm Forbes will tell you about the politician who came to visit him one day and made so little impression that he wasn't even invited to sign the visitors' book. His familiar face turned up later in the White House – as President Jimmy Carter!

Defying that tradition of sons who are never the men their fathers were, Malcolm took the silver spoon out of his mouth and used it to expand Bertie's successful enterprise out of all recognition, moving from publishing into real estate and counting among his personal properties the Governor's Palace in Morocco, the magnificent Château Balleroy in France, an island in the South Pacific, a private Boeing 727 decked out as a flying mansion and, perhaps most valued of all, more Fabergé eggs than the whole priceless collection within the Kremlin of Moscow.

When he is not flying in that Boeing or sailing on the *Highlander*, you will find him chalking up more records for hot-air ballooning across America or riding his motor-bike (he owns the company) to Moscow or Peking. But if any of that gives an impression of a spend-thrift playboy then nothing could be further from the truth. Malcolm Forbes is a shrewd financial adviser with a genius for making money, believing in the philosophy that you must spend a lot to make more.

The financial ear of his magazine is close to the ground and the authority of its writers commands enormous attention. Malcolm Forbes himself is not prepared to stop short of a practical example. He once bought 250 square miles of Colorado, intending to turn it into a game reserve for the state. But the Attorney General put so many obstacles in his path that he eventually gave up the idea and sold off 30 per cent of it – for twenty million pounds.

His idyllic island in the South Pacific, called Laucala, is not only a splendid retreat where the natives line up to welcome him but is also an island of copra, the seed which gives us coconut oil. (Needless to say, he bought the place when copra was at a low price.)

With his son Christopher – there are four sons and a daughter – he set out to build a collection of Victorian paintings when they were out of fashion. Today, when they are back in vogue, he has the largest private collection in the world.

To reach Malcolm Forbes in that Fifth Avenue building you pass bullet-proof displays of those priceless Fabergé eggs, as well as Abraham Lincoln's lum-hat, the opera glasses which fell from his hands at Ford's Theatre, Washington, in 1865, when he was assassinated by the actor John Wilkes Booth – and a piece of towel they used to wipe away the President's blood.

But acquisition does nothing to divert his central philosophy that life has to be fun. 'When you're alive – LIVE' is one of his favourite sayings, incorporated in a book of epigrams which he once published under the tongue-in-cheek title *The Sayings of Chairman Malcolm*. Though his father came more and more to Scotland in his latter years, Malcolm's own connection became fairly tenuous in the post-war period, such was his involvement with life in the United States.

In time, however, I began to sense that advancing years were turning his thoughts more and more to his father's homeland, arousing a greater appreciation of the character and determination it must have taken to follow that route from a lowly cottage near New Deer to the skyscrapers of New York.

He has been known to slip quietly across Scotland on his motor-bike, and just a few years ago he flew into Aberdeen Airport hoping to buy Castle Forbes, which lies at the other end of Aberdeenshire from where his own humble father had grown up and which was then available for purchase. He failed to do business with Lord Forbes but links were nevertheless re-established.

In the mid-seventies his daughter Moira came to spend two years at Aberdeen University, living at the halls of residence at Seaton and visiting Whitehill, where she met some of the people who still remembered her grandfather.

Whatever his thoughts about strengthening the ties with his father's native land, however, Malcolm Forbes had been dicing with death too often for the comfort of his insurance advisers, whether at war, at sea or in his beloved balloons, where he twice came within seconds of being killed. But his closest shave of all came on Sunday, 10 July 1971, when the King of Morocco invited him, as owner of the Governor's Palace, to his birthday party. King Hassan and his guests were about to start lunch when 1,200 military cadets came hurtling up the Casablanca road and swung into the palace gates, automatics ablaze with gunfire. Malcolm Forbes thought the fireworks display had started a little prematurely. Little did he know it was the beginning of an attempted *coup d'état*. Soon there was a bedlam of gunfire, screams and spurting blood and, by the time the dust had settled, 100 people lay slaughtered in the courtyard. The Belgian ambassador died in the arms of the French ambassador and the famous French cardiologist, Jean Himbert, was callously machine-gunned to death as he tried to crawl to the aid of the wounded.

The King had escaped and the resourceful Malcolm Forbes leaped over a wall to the sand and crawled away on his belly. Eventually he was found by the soldiers, marched back to the palace and forced to lie among the others, in fear and doubt about the future of his existence.

Providence, it seemed, was on his side and the horrifying experience did not deter him from making plans for the Arab world. In fact he followed up by printing an edition of *Forbes* in Arabic. There were only a few hundred potential readers but those few were worth so many tens of billions that there was an absolute rush to buy advertising space.

Perhaps it was the smeddum of an Aberdeenshire parentage that saw him through that emergency in Morocco, along with many others, proving him not only a winner but a survivor in the most literal sense. For him it is all a great adventure.

These thoughts were passing through my head that July afternoon of 1986 as I sat in the balcony of the Mitchell Hall and watched a graduation ceremony which would have filled Bertie Forbes with pride. Just as he had gone forth to make his mark on America and to be fêted and honoured by the University of Southern California, his own son was now back in the home corner of the Forbeses, just thirty miles from that

Cunnyknowe cottage at Whitehill of New Deer. When the ceremony had spilled out into the quadrangle of Marischal College and the greetings and congratulations had been well and truly bestowed, Malcolm Forbes took me aside and asked if I would help to fulfil a wish which had been welling up inside him.

More than thirty years after the death of his father, he wanted to revive the tradition of 'Bertie's Picnic', out there at Whitehill where the old school was now converted into a dwelling house but where there was still a recognizable community of local families, with children now attending the village schools at New Deer, Maud and New Pitsligo.

I contacted Mrs Glennie and her parents' committee at Whitehill and they were delighted to make the local arrangements. So it was, in the summer of 1987, that Malcolm Forbes set out from his office on Fifth Avenue, New York, to board his luxurious Boeing 727 at Newark Airport for the flight to Scotland. From Aberdeen he drove out into the Buchan territory of the North-East, wending his way to that rural corner of Whitehill, in the parish of New Deer, where the children of his father's old homeland were waiting to greet him with their own special song of welcome. Bertie's Picnic had now become Malcolm's Picnic.

The man whose personal wealth is counted in hundreds of millions of pounds, who grew to be one of America's most fabulous characters and might well have been one of its finest Presidents, had brought the story full circle; back to the neep parks of Buchan and the humble cottage of the Cunnyknowe where, once upon a time, this fairy-tale began.

CHAPTER TWENTY-NINE

◆◇◆

My Heritage Trail

So life wears on, and in the early spring of '87 I went for a drive around Buchan, as if to redefine my boundaries and confirm in my own mind that the land of my begetting was still there in all its rich tang of expression.

As I drove out from the Saplinbrae House Hotel I paused along the road at the Abbey of Deer, spiritual heart of Buchan with its ancient stones still clinging together after eight centuries, the foundations laid out in the form of a cross, its spruce and beech and ancient elms standing stiff as guardsmen o'er their historic keep. Then I wandered across the burn and up through the gorse and heather of Aikey Brae, the hillside much quarried by uncaring councils, the trees now legally vandalized by some visiting woodchopper.

By an even stretch an old tinker's wagon seemed poised for the Sunday fair while, on brown carpets of spring soil, tractors laid the seed of a new growth, trailing a procession of gulls over there by the shelter of Pitfour estate. Spring cattle dotted the greensward in shades of black and brown while the sheep munched happily near by and the burn went warbling on its way to the great North Sea, to a counterpoint of gentle breeze.

Up through Maud I drove, and out by the old Brucklay road, where daffodils spread their bloom against beech hedge.

On I went by my grandfather's former tenancy at Mains of Whitehill, down Pisga, along by Mac's Yard, past the moss and up the Gairdner's Brae into New Pitsligo, or Kyak as I knew it; at the far end of the village, little hoosies which once had thackit roofs now sheltered under brittle slate. So the road marched high by Windyheads, where the Civil Aviation Authority has an air traffic control, a bare hill that gives sight of Troup Head then dips towards Pennan, where weekend crowds

179

now flock to view the setting of David Puttnam's popular film, *Local Hero*.

On by New Aberdour, where the sea wafts up with its own rich tang of dilse, and round to that magnificent stretch of golden sand at Fraserburgh, where two prancing horses materialized like magic and were ridden headlong into the sea to cool their heated hooves. Even David Puttnam could not have produced a more timely and picturesque scene. Round by the rocky foreshore, towards the harbour, I remembered the lifeboat disaster of February, 1953, just nine days after the Great Gale which devastated the North-East in that Coronation year. There we had stood, helpless, as Coxswain Andrew Ritchie thrashed his way towards survival, only to be beaten at the last minute by a piece of flotsam which finally tore out his strength.

Along by Crimond, two siccar chiels leaned defiantly on a gate-post, wondering no doubt who the stranger might be as I tarried and remembered my father-in-law, Nelson Keith, and his brother Norman, products of the crofting community here between the shadows of Mormond Hill and the shores of St Combs. In this parish kirk of Crimond, their father had sung as a young lad with Jessie Seymour Irvine, the local minister's daughter who wrote the famous psalm tune for the twenty-third that spread the name of Crimond around the world.

You could hear it now, rich and mellow in its choral cry, lingering long past the generation that heard it first but coming from the past as a voice that will endure and tell us of the universal faith and hope that sustains mankind through the trauchles of the daily darg.

CHAPTER THIRTY

Back to Culsh

Yes, the land was still there all right, deep and abiding in the regeneration of its tilth, serving one generation after another, furrow upon furrow of the human flesh. The landscapes are undeniably the same as we remember from our childhood days, yet you could swear there was a difference in substance; for sure there is a difference in the emotions they evoke within the human breast. The transformation, we must conclude, is within ourselves.

Layers of experience which build themselves into the fabric of a human life will alter our standpoint one way or another. Time will edge us onward upon that long and winding road, each mile and bend of the way producing its own glint of sunlight or cast of cloud, arousing in the human soul a subtle change of feeling.

Even along this short, absorbing tour of Buchan, by the time I had reached the sandy shores of Cruden Bay, the bleak Hills of Fisherie were already a world away in my emotional experience, dim in the mists of an antiquity which is eerie to behold and impossible to explain.

Driving in through Longside, Mintlaw and Old Deer, I came round the Hill of Clackriach from Aikey Brae once more, as the valley of Maud unrolled itself before my wondering gaze.

Across the howe lay Honeyneuk, now in the hands of Jim and Belinda Muir, who ran the place themselves, eident, hard-working folk. The Websters were now taking their place alongside the Pauls and the Raes and the Galls and all the forgotten folk who had farmed down the years at Honeyneuk, each in their day regarding the place as a home and living and way of life vital unto that moment and familiar in every neuk, little anticipating that one day they would be consigned, like all the others, to a faded name on a title deed.

There stood the cottar houses, no longer providing the labour of the land, bare grey relics of a rural life now lacking an authentic core. Gone, it seemed to me, was the warmth of the farming community I had known; gone the structure that made it so. If all the world were truly a stage, as the Bard maintained, then gone were the cast of this particular rural drama, exit left and right, to leave a proscenium that echoed still with the sounds of a performance long faded into the wings and never to be repeated.

I was remembering about folk like old Jimmy Park, the bailie at Honeyneuk when my father took on the place, a man who spent his days in undistinguished bliss and typified as well as any the kind of folk who vrocht the grudging acres of Buchan. Old Jimmy lived in the cottar house with the 'aul 'umman', which was I suppose the nearest he ever came to an endearment; but it had a good deal more depth than all the 'dears' and 'darlings' that fall so loosely from smarter lips. Jimmy and the aul 'umman raised five strapping sons and taught them nothing very much to catch the modern fancy.

But they showed them by example how to be thrifty, hard-working, honest, decent members of society, and two of them grew up to be fine, reliable farm servants like their father while two more solid lads became prison warders and the fifth boy died in the heat of the Second War. I doubt if Jimmy and his wife ever got over it but the sorrow was not for public viewing. A quiet tear was wiped away and at yokin' time he was down the greip as usual to muck out and feed the nowt, with a spit or a curse about the pipe that wouldn't draw and, in time, the deep rumble of a laugh.

Jimmy Park was Santa Claus with the robes off, a finely creased face of good humour and character and above all kindliness, a man untroubled by education and not much the worse for it as far as I could see. With steady gait he roamed free among those nowt in the fields and found that rare peace which comes of being at one with nature. About Hogmanay his gait was less steady for Jimmy would repair to the local 'Refresh' at the railway station, where Lil and Lena would serve his celebration 'fusky' and at closing time his fellow servants would prop him up to face a world that had gone damnably off balance. He would wipe the bree from his big moustache and reflect on the pleasures of simply being alive. The taste was as plain as the Moss o' Byth and the gratitude and satisfaction as deep as the wreath of snow by the windmill at Honeyneuk.

There are folk who would scoff at such human beings but they had a wealth of their own which eluded the more sophisticated; not the affluence of material things but just the priceless currency of a generous humanity.

I doubt if Jimmy Park knew much about the inside of a kirk but the faith of the man was there in his eyes. And as his image springs unaccountably to mind at this particular moment, I have little doubt that he found his eternity in the corner of some Elysian Field where he tends the Lord's cattle and puffs out yoams of satisfaction from the short stem of his Steenhive.

From Honeyneuk I took the scenic route by the Fishfir Brae and the Brucklay policies to the West Lodge, turning left and then right to mount the gentle Hill of Culsh, where I find myself drawn time and time again in a manner which might suggest my eventual destination. There I stood pondering by the gravestone of my great-grandfather, Gavin Greig, the outstanding Buchan figure of his day, whose obituary notice in 1914 filled whole text-size pages of the local papers.

The departure from this earthly scene while still in his fifties brought an agonized cry from the heart of his many admirers.

'Gavin Greig dead. That was the news and it struck his friends like the announcement of a lost battle,' was how the editor of the *Peterhead Sentinel* began his seven long columns. I still have a copy of the paper. He eulogized a man who, from the remoteness of Buchan, had not only written plays, poetry and music which reached the far corners of the country but had gathered the folk songs of the land to a degree which gained the recognition of professors in Berlin.

All the time, while he and Granny Greig were bringing up

their nine children, he was also managing to turn learning in the classrooms of Whitehill School into a joyous adventure. Ill health was bearing in upon him but the editor of the *Sentinel* gave us some hint of the man through his letters, which are often a reliable guide to the inner self:

Mr Greig caused his pupils to love himself and to love learning. When illness and weakness came upon him it was very unwillingly that he abandoned the various helpful agencies in which he had been engaged. This was touchingly revealed to me in the letter which he wrote from Deeside announcing his inability to continue his articles on the Bards. 'This I regret very much indeed; but I have found it necessary to lighten the ship and have been laying down one task after another, to see if vacuity will help me to recover tone and form.'

The letter is almost too sacred for quotation; but in order that our readers may see the noble spirit in which this man laboured in our midst let me extract one paragraph. 'Of course, though thus in a way driven to discontinue the series meantime on the account of the state of my health, I should like very much to resume the task at some future date ... I do trust you will see how I am placed and grant me kindly indulgence. Believe me, my dear friend, the will remains as strong as ever. If the flesh is weak I must e'en submit. Honestly, when I breathe a wish for restored vigour, it is that I may be able to do a little more work in our little world and I should think we ought to be ashamed to put forward any other plea.'

The versatility of the man was most amazing. And what a companion he was! If his oratory at times touched the sublime it could also at other times be full of exquisite humour. The best instance of this I can recall is the speech he gave at the complimentary dinner to Dr James F. Tocher on the occasion of his leaving Peterhead to take up the post of county analyst. There was much good oratory on that occasion and, as I remarked at the time, the speech of Mr

Greig was the speech of the evening. He was entrusted with the toast of 'Peterhead'. Such a blending of fine feeling with delightful humour is seldom found and it was no wonder that those of us favoured to listen were quite enraptured.

CHAPTER THIRTY-ONE

— ◦◦ —

Rock of Ages

As I stood by Gavin Greig's gravestone now I tried to conjure up the scene of his funeral day, on Thursday, 3 September 1914, assisted once more by the pages of the *Sentinel*, whose editor gave this account of that sad occasion, improving our understanding of what a country funeral was like in those distant days:

It was indeed a Buchan funeral. From far and near the mourners had gathered. Almost every mode of conveyance had been called into requisition. Of course the country gig predominated; but there was a strong representation of motor cars, big and small. The service was specially impressive by its simplicity. The benches [of the school] were filled with adult mourners and many others could only get standing room. From the schoolhouse near at hand the coffin had been carried and was placed on a white-covered table. Handsome in polished oak and brass, it was unusually long for our departed friend was a tall man. The drawing back of the glass partition enabled the school to be used as a single meeting hall. In such a place on such an occasion one could not help musing. This was where he had reigned. For so many years this had been the centre of his beneficent activities. Here his kindly guidance had started many a scholar on the acquisition of knowledge, bringing them later on to see that wisdom was greater than knowledge.

A poor building to look at, yes, but it had been ennobled by the life of him that laboured in it so long. It had, too, deep and tender and sacred memories. Today's funeral was not the first that had set forth from this place. There was an occasion when a smaller coffin had been carried forth after a service which, even now, years later, was recalled with hushed voices by those who had been present at it. Then a daughter of the schoolhouse had been cut off in youthful charm and he whose weary frame now lay in that oaken casket had himself played the accompaniment to the funeral hymn.

The hymn now sung was 'Rock of Ages'. Could a better choice have been made? Most popular of the sacred songs in our tongue, it linked us to many a hallowed memory. And he whom we had come to lay to rest was skilled above most in sacred music and familiar with the songs of Zion. It was fitting too that the scripture passages should have been read by the Rev. J. B. Duncan of Lynturk, who has been so closely associated with Mr Greig in the work of collecting and editing the Folk Songs of the North-East.

Some of the words of Sacred Writ sent our minds off at a tangent. 'The days of our years are three score years and ten.' Alas, if only this had been true of our departed friend, would our regret have been so great? What might he not have accomplished if another dozen years had been vouchsafed to him? But the wise Taskmaster had ordered it otherwise and He doeth all things well.

The Rev. William Beveridge's prayer had some beautiful touches. We rendered God thanks for what our friend had been and for the faithfulness to the gift bestowed upon him. It was a short service but simple and telling.

The accompaniment to the hymn was played by Miss Dingwall-Fordyce of Brucklay Castle. The cortège set forth on its slow funeral way to the Churchyard of Culsh, New Deer. In the school playground we left the mourning scholars, drawn up in one long line, under the supervision of Mr A. R. Dunbar, the comrade of Mr Greig in many a venture, the prototype of 'Mains' in the plays which bid fair to do most to perpetuate his literary fame and now, by a strange coincidence, the *locum tenens* to take up the work of teaching, which death has compelled his friend to close.

Before the eulogies and colourful descriptions were completed, we had read that two well-known local farmers, Mr James Brebner of Hillhead of Ironside and Mr William Shirras, Upper Ironside, had an alarming experience while attending the funeral. When descending the brae at Weetingshill, the horse in their trap slipped and fell. It rose with such force that the shafts and part of the trap broke away. Mr Brebner jumped on to the bank at the roadside but Mr Shirras was precipitated with great violence under the vehicle quite close to the horse's feet. The animal took fright and bolted along the road, dragging with it part of the trap. The vehicles in front were now in danger and several of the occupants jumped on to the road and were successful in turning the horse to the side.

The animal made a dash for the wire paling but got entangled and was captured. Except for cuts and bruises, Mr Shirras escaped what could have been a tragic accident.

The pall-bearers included my grandfather, Arthur Barron, Mains of Whitehill (Gavin Greig's son-in-law), Tom Rodger from Crimond (son-in-law), Ernest Coutts from Port Elphinstone (another son-in-law, soon to be killed in the First World War), James Ferguson of Glasgow (brother-in-law), A. W. Simpson of Monymusk (brother-in-law) and James Will, schoolmaster at New Pitsligo.

I make no apology for reproducing the list of mourners, which not only testifies to the diligence of the reporting journalist but gives an interesting picture of the names which constituted the Buchan scene at the outbreak of the First World War. More than seventy years later those same names still survive in their descendants and, if this book is read in another seventy years, it should be of some interest to see how well the indigenous families of Buchan have adhered to their roots.

Here then is that catalogue of country folk who followed my great-grandfather to the Hill of Culsh at the outbreak of a war,

the prospect of which so depressed him as to further dim the
flame which flickered precariously between life and death:

W. F. Anton, schoolmaster, Crimond; James Angus, Queen
Street, Peterhead; A. Adams, merchant, New Deer; James
Alexander, Affath; A. J. Allan, banker, Maud; Rev. W.
Beveridge, New Deer; Joseph Blake, New Pitsligo; James
Brebner, Hillhead of Ironside; John Barron, Cabra, Mintlaw.

George Brebner, Mill of Whitehill; Mr Blake, Fyvie;
W. Barron, Whitehill; Alex Barron, Whitehill; Rev. Wm
Cowie, Maud; Henry Cowie, Schoolhouse, New Deer;
George Cruickshank, factor, Fyvie Estates; P. Creighton,
banker, New Deer; Archibald Campbell, Auchmunziel,
New Deer; George Calvert, roads superintendent, Maud;
Mr Catto, Mains of Culsh; George Corbett, Weetingshill;
James Cruickshank, Grassiehill; B. Cheyne, South Culsh;
Mr Corsie, Peterhead; L. Cruden, Brucklay Castle; Rev. J.
B. Duncan, Lynturk; D. C. Dundas, schoolmaster, Inveral-
lochy; Adam R. Dunbar, retired schoolmaster, New Deer;
Mr Davidson, Gaval; John Duffus, New Pitsligo; Charles
Davidson, Waulkmill.

Ex-Baillie George Duncan, Peterhead; James Elrick,
Aucheoch; George Fowlie, Mains of Auchreddie; J. Fowlie,
Millhill; J. Ferguson, Aberdeen; John Fowlie, Loanhead;
John Forbes, Mill of Fedderate; James Findlay, Kirkhill; W.
Findlay, Peterhead; Rev. D. Grigor, Congregational
Church, New Deer; Mr Giles, Fyvie; Keith Gray, Brucklay
Castle; A. Gillespie, New Deer; Mr Gordon, Middlemuir,
Methlick; Rev. J. Halliday, Peterhead; William Hadden,
schoolmaster, Knaven; William Halkett, Peterhead;
Edward P. Horne, New Deer; Alex Horne, New Deer;
James Ironside, Brunthill; Mr Ironside, schoolmaster, Fet-
ternear; John Innes, Port Elphinstone; John Jack, Rathen;
James Johnston, Mill of Allathan; Joseph Johnston, Fri-
dayhill; James Knox, Peterhead; M. Keith, Aberdour
House, factor Brucklay estates; Alex Keith, Burnshangie;
R. Murdoch Lawrence, Aberdeen; Rev. W. M. Meston, UF

Church, New Pitsligo; Captain J. Morrison, 5th Battalion, Gordon Highlanders, Maud; Frank Metcalfe, Cachar, India; Wm Mitchell, New Deer; John Mitchell, Millbrex; John Mowat, Craigmaud; James Morrison, schoolmaster, Oldwhat.

William Murison, Upper Aucheoch; William Mitchell, Whitecairns; Dr Mitchell, New Deer; Alex Milne, Maud; J. Michie, Maud; Alex Murray, Hillhead, Bonnykelly; James Moir, Fedderate; James Macpherson, schoolmaster, Cairnbanno; James McAllan, Whitebog; Rev. R. MacKinlay, Congregational Church, New Pitsligo; J. McBoyle, Fyvie; Alex R. McFarlane, editor, *Peterhead Sentinel*; J. Pettie, Port Elphinstone; C. D. Rice, rector, Peterhead Academy; Mr Ritchie, retired schoolmaster, Port Elphinstone; John Reid, Colliegard; George Robertson, clerk to school board, New Pitsligo; A. Robb, Brucklay Castle; William Shirras, Upper Ironside; Dufton Scott, Inverurie; J. Stephen, schoolmaster, New Deer; George Stewart, Auchmaleddie; Mr Smith, Burnshangie; A. Smith, banker, Inverurie; J. Boyes Sinclair, merchant, New Pitsligo; J. Sim, New Deer; A. MacDonald Reid, Central School, Peterhead; J. F. Tocher, County Analyst, Aberdeen; R. Topping, HM Inspector of Schools; William Turner, butler, Brucklay Castle; James Will, schoolmaster, New Pitsligo; George Watt, Whinhill; David Will, Alehousehill; Charles S. Walker, Brucklay; William Walker, 65 Argyll Place, Aberdeen; Dr Wood, Longside; James Walker, Brucklay Castle.

CHAPTER THIRTY-TWO

End of the Day

That solid body of menfolk – for women did not follow the hearse in those departed days – came round from the School of Whitehill, down past Weetingshill and along by Mains of Fedderate, turning right, as I had done that very day, to ascend the slopes of Culsh. In their solemn ranks, they gathered round the spot where now I stood alone contemplating the fact that each one of them, in their appointed time, had since come down the same road, or one like it. As far as I know, the last survivor of that vast cortège was Jimmy Moir, who died a centenarian not so long ago, having been blacksmith at Whitehill and a cousin of the same Bertie Forbes who went to America and became a millionaire.

As I paid homage at Gavin Greig's grave, I remembered again those newspapers which carried not only detailed accounts of his remarkable career but even swatches of poetry composed on the spur of the moment in his honour. One which appeared in the *Aberdeen Daily Journal* perhaps summed up what the others were trying to say:

> Gone from our gaze; but never lost, thy work
> Abides, diffusing like the sun its rays
> Of light and strength to all that can receive
> Its powerful influence. On great and small
> Thy varied gifts were showered with lavish hand
>
> In music's art thou showed'st a master's hand
> Uniting both the gifts of sight and sound
> In later days the folk-song of the swain
> In thousand songs and tunes obeyed thy spell
> Detracting from our rush and love of gain

Thou broughtest back to mind the freer life
Of old, the happy childlike days of men
And settings, too, in book-form thou did'st give
And realistic placed the deeds of men
Dramatically in 'Mains' and 'Mains Again'.

Athletic body first and mind always
Endued with genius rare; thy facile pen
Has left its mark embedded in our hearts
Another tree branch lopped from Scotia's bard*
Like him thou'st lived too much and died too soon

High up here on the Hill of Culsh the nights are stretching
their arms to embrace the fledgling spring; the seeds of a life
renewed are sprouting in the virgin soil of those Buchan fields
spread out before me now. Though the years have cast their
shadows and borne away those people who inhabited the childhood dream, I am strangely at one with the world on this lonely
hillside; just as I was not so long ago on the heights of Mount
Nebo, where Moses came to die, and I could look across the
Jordan Valley to the Dead Sea and the Judean Hills beyond,
with Jericho brooding in the middle distance, all still and
timeless and unchanged from long before the days of the Lord.

This twentieth century itself may be running into old age,
but at the first melodious call of an April evening the heart still
stirs with the eternal hope of youth – and the sheer privilege
and joy of being alive to partake of this mystifying and glorious
adventure.

* The allusion here is to Greig's family kinship with Burns.